My Shadows of Death

Joy Forgan Burney
Ps. 63:7

With my love

MY
SHADOWS
of DEATH

Lessons Learned in the Valley

JOY FORGAN BURNEY

XULON PRESS

Xulon Press
2301 Lucien Way #415
Maitland, FL 32751
407.339.4217
www.xulonpress.com

Scripture quotations taken from the King James Version (KJV) – *public domain*.

Edited by Xulon Press.

Printed in the United States of America.

ISBN-13: 9781545634868

Yea, though I walk through the valley of the shadow of death, I will fear no evil: for thou art with me. – Psalms 23:4

But I would ye should understand, brethren, that the things which happened unto me have fallen out rather unto the furtherance of the gospel; So that my bonds in Christ are manifest in all the palace, and in all other places. –Philippians 1:12-13

Table of Contents

Forward

Sometimes we have the privilege of reading after someone who writes from the reservoir of an entire life's experience. The good times and the difficult ones, the mountain tops and the valleys. In clear and compelling language, Joy Burney shares the biblical blueprint for trusting God during those ever-changing seasons of life. It has been my honor to be Joy's pastor for over 10 years. I know that you will be captivated by her journey and challenged to trust God more even in the midst of your darkest valleys!

Frank Carl, Pastor, Genoa Baptist Church

Introduction

This book has been difficult to write. In these pages, I write about life lessons I have gained to help others find God in their own experiences. This is actually a mini auto-biography.

Mine has been a life of some difficult events. I suffered sexual abuse by a trusted teacher as a child and dealt with perfectionism and anxiety as an adult. Transparency has always been important to me. Every life includes both joy and sorrow, and I have decided to share both. I must admit that penning a few of these events has been challenging. I wonder what will people think and say of my choices; I wonder if they will appreciate or scorn my transparency.

As I share the hurtful parts of my life, I do not mean to dredge up things from the past, but instead to share with you what God has taught me from them. My prayer in life is "Lord, even if one." If one life might be impacted and touched by this book, then it will be worth all the fear that I have gone through to putting it out there for all to see and read. The book's purpose is to point others to the One Who can take me (and us) down this road, and that is Jesus. Philippians 3:10 says, "That I may know Him, and the power of

His resurrection, and the fellowship of His sufferings, being made conformable unto His death." If we want to enjoy the power of His resurrection, we must be willing to go through suffering also.

Psalm 23:4 reads, "Yea thou I walk thru the valley of the shadow of death, I will fear no evil for Thou art with me." What follows in this book are the "shadows" of death in my life that I am sharing. Shadows will not and cannot hurt you, but they might cause you fear or make you anxious. They might also cause you to hurt because of the lesson being taught to you during the shadow.

My story is a story of a Love that would not let me go, a Hope that was always present even if not seen, a life hid in Christ, and a Faith-filled assurance even when I felt helpless. Here are some scenes from my story—my life—and how God has been with me as I walked through the valley of my "shadows of death." May you look at your story (for we all have one) and see what God is doing and has done in and through you.

My life story is to tell you of Christ.

Once we are born, we begin to go down the path of the valley of the shadow of death, for death will come to all. The various situations that are brought into our life as we travel this path will shape our life for eternity. Death is a necessary part of life. We all experience many deaths and resurrections both during life here on earth and finally, thanks to Jesus, the final death and resurrection. Each life experiences many deaths and resurrections before we leave for our eternal heavenly Home. Some of the deaths I have experienced on this earth were for my correction, some for my perfection. All of them were to mold me into the image of

Christ and prepare me for Heaven. Romans 8:28-29 says, "And we know that all things work together for good to them that love God, to them who are the called according to his purpose. For whom he did foreknow, he also did predestinate to be conformed to the image of his Son, that he might be the firstborn among many brethren."

I have lived a very full life filled with happiness (or "joy"). I really do not like the word happiness as God never promised us a life of happiness (even Jesus wept). Rather, He has promised us a life of joy and peace even in the midst of shadows. What makes you happy, might not make me happy, but joy is available to all. Joy is not dependent on circumstances, unlike happiness. Joy is a choice in how we react to life's uncertainties with faith in God. That being said, since my name is Joy according to the poem my Mother wrote for me, " Danny, a name picked for a boy, but a beautiful girl must be named Joy," it seems funny saying a life of "Joy" unless I make it a lower-case (j)oy. A life of joy, fun, adventures, accomplishments, contentment, sorrow, trials, temptations and testings. A life of deep pain but also a life of deep blessings, a life of brokenness. It is a life of shadows of the valley of death; some deaths are good, others are deaths that God allowed me to go through for the purpose of brokenness. I often wondered in life why I was called upon to suffer some of these deaths, but I believe now that God has given me a ministry of brokenness so that others may see Christ. I have seen brokenness explained in this way: "The result of God's providential pressure that brings the believer to give up any attempt to live and cope apart from the indwelling Christ" (John 12:24). Quote by John Woodward of Grace Fellowship International.

My beginning, though, was blessed. 2 Corinthians 4:17-18 reads:

> "For our light affliction, which is but for a moment, worketh for us a far more exceeding and eternal weight of glory; While we look not at the things which are seen, but at the things which are not seen: for the things which are seen are temporal; but the things which are not seen are eternal."

A look at me today does not reveal what I have suffered. I pray you would not see or focus on what I have suffered through sexual abuse, loss, anxiety, and depression along with physical pain and being a pastor's wife through most of this! Instead, I pray you see the sufficiency of Christ through these words. I pray you see one ordinary woman under the direction of an Extraordinary God through faith and perseverance, running the race to win. In my life, I have chosen not to compete, but to complete my walk to bring honor and glory to Christ. I believe that God, even in the dark times, is accomplishing this pursuit.

I am reminded as I write this of the song composed by John Bunyan Herbert that says:

> *Jesus walked this lonesome valley*
> *He had to walk it by Himself*
> *Oh, nobody else could walk it for Him*
> *He had to walk it by Himself.*

You must walk this lonesome valley
You have to walk it by yourself
Oh, nobody else can walk it for you
You have to walk it by yourself.

Even though I was surrounded by others and even a great cloud of witnesses, the journey was mine to walk. The following were my valleys, they were my shadows of death. But in each death, resurrection— new life—followed.

Chapter 1

The Death of Sin

My parents' loving example remains a cherished personal heritage. I lived a happy childhood with my parents, Harry Wilson Forgan Sr. and Beulah Pearl Myers Forgan. The lessons they taught me, in word and deed, their smiles, love, and sacrifice for me, my sister, Carol Ann and my brother, Harry Jr. are immeasurable. Both siblings were older than me: Carol Ann by nearly ten years and Harry Jr. by five.

My Forgan Family

Our family was a church-going one. We gathered around as Carol Ann played an old upright piano and the family sang hymn after hymn. Our family life was filled with activities like singing, laughing, root beer or cherry floats around the table, playing games, home cooked meals, visiting others, family reunions, work, chores, play and vacations. (I really loved staying for a week in a red caboose and camping at Clays Park outside of Massillon.) All of our family days were full.

Root Beer Floats around the table with Mom and Dad

Playing dress up and of course, a doll baby

Some of my fondest childhood memories include: playing dress up, appreciating my doll babies, tap and toe dancing lessons with Eleanor Von Wyl, piano lessons with Mrs. McClure, and growing up in Forgan's Grocery, the corner grocery owned and operated by my parents.

Forgan's Grocery

I fondly remember delivering groceries to some of our elderly customers and a blind man. The neighborhood was a common middle-class neighborhood where everyone looked out for each other. I was very carefree and happy, loving the scenes along the way of the houses and landscapes. Since my parents owned the corner grocery store, I knew most all the neighbors. None of the routes were far away. I do not remember how old I was when I started helping my parents in this way except to know I was safe; I really never feared. When I went to the blind man's house, I would knock on the door and holler "Grocery Girl." I would always go inside and unpack and put away his groceries. Another couple I delivered to would often give me two stalks of rhubarb; their yummy gift always made me so happy. I would run home, give them to my mother, and wait for her to cook them up for me with lots of sugar, which was so tasty!

When I was younger, my parents would stand me up on the ice-cream counter of their grocery store and have me sing to the customers. I sang to the city bus riders too, when my dad was the driver.

In the store, I learned to serve others and treat everyone with kindness and respect. For each customer, we would take out a large brown paper bag and write down the prices of their items as they brought them to the counter. Then, when they were all finished shopping, I had to stand in front of the customer and add up the total without a calculator! Some of the customers shopped for two weeks of goods, so the numbers were long. We used a big old-fashioned cash register. It was my job to punch in the total amount of the customers' groceries; when it dinged and the drawer opened, I had to count out their change to them!

I loved all the delivery people who brought our inventory. The bread men, milk men, meat and cheese delivery men were all wonderful. They would bring me doll babies and help me cross the street to Emerson elementary school. We had a penny-candy counter and I remember my parents' patience as they stood for however long it took for a child with five pennies to pick out five pieces of candy.

My dad also worked at Republic Steel in Massillon as times were rough and finances lean, even though I never knew that. Mom and I often worked the late night at the store and then would go pick up Dad. One night when we did not have to pick up Dad, I was so tired, that I set the store clock ahead one hour so Mom and I could go home early. Well, I forgot about the big clock uptown that we always passed on the way home. When Mother saw that clock, needless to say, I was in big trouble! But we did get home earlier that night.

I had a total of 101 doll babies (most of them gifts from others). Every Christmas, we would bathe them all, wash their outfits, and comb their hair. Then, we would set them up all around the room. I lived in the days when doctors made house calls, and I used to get strep throat often. Dr. Browarsky would come up to my room, look at all my dolls, tell me to roll over as he filled his long needle with a double dose of penicillin. He always said the same thing to divert my attention: "You have more dolls than Carter's has little liver pills." He would then inject the needle, and I fell for it every time!

I always took a doll to church, especially on Sunday nights, and sat her up beside me in the church pew. Attending Sunday evening church each week, even at the age of eight years old, was expected. One Sunday night was different though. The difference happened at the end of the message. Pastor Douglas Eades of First Baptist Church in Massillon, Ohio gave an invitation for anyone to come forward with any decision for Christ. I walked forward to an old-fashioned altar and told the pastor I was coming to let everyone know I had accepted Christ into my heart as my Savior. I wanted to make my decision public.

> "For the wages of sin is death; but the gift
> of God is eternal life through Jesus Christ
> our Lord" (Romans 6:23).

I had accepted the free gift of salvation.

My Mother had both shared and taught me God's salvation plan in the home and the children's church that she taught every Sunday. I believe my child's heart was toward God from the beginning through the godly home I was brought up in. There was never any question that God would not be first in my young life after all He had done for me. You cannot become a Christian by being raised in a godly home; you must make that decision on your own. Even all of her teaching did not prepare me for the thrill of accepting Christ as my very own. I do believe, however, that your heart may be influenced by a godly home, and I am very thankful that I grew up in one.

That evening was the first death I had ever experienced in my young life. It was the death of sin. Oh, I have sinned many times since that day, but that was the day, I accepted the sacrifice Christ had made for me on the cross to pay for my sin. You see the shadow of death came over the cross when Jesus died. I realized that even at the age of eight I was a sinner who needed a Savior, and Christ had paid the price for me. It was then that I came to the cross to accept Christ as my Savior for salvation, and I have never been the same since that day. When Christ takes over your heart, all things become new. There is a song that says, "Oh, I never shall forget that day, when Jesus washed my sins away, and He can do the same for you."

That day, I confessed that I was a sinner, believed that Christ died on the cross to pay the price for my sin, and asked Christ to come into my life and be my Savior. I then followed the Lord in the obedience of baptism. At my church, we attended classes for a few weeks to help us understand what baptism was, which I think was so very good. Baptism is an outward expression of what had taken place inside of me. Through baptism, I was sharing with others that the old Joy had died to the power of sin over me, and I was then raised in newness of life to walk the path Christ had for me.

I am so glad my parents were so loving and kind to show me the way and not to hinder me from accepting Christ and walking in His ways but instead encouraged me. The Bible says in Luke 17:2: "It were better for him that a millstone were hanged about his neck, and he cast into the sea, than that he should offend one of these little ones"

After that decision for Christ, everything was different. I never wanted to take my doll with me to church anymore. Not that taking them was wrong. I still loved my dolls, but I just did not need them there anymore. I wanted to concentrate more on the teaching and preaching, so I might learn more about Jesus. Even Easter and Christmas were much more meaningful now that I knew Jesus was alive in me! I loved sitting with my family for those special services. I became very active in many of the various ministries of the church including guild girls, youth groups, missions, and music groups. I became keenly aware of the testimony I was portraying to others of Jesus. I also longed to share the salvation message with anyone who would hear me.

Yes, Christ can do the same for you. Will you bow your head right now, and choose Christ? You are the only one who may make that eternal decision. God has no grandchildren; we are all first born.

Did you know that in Hebrews 9:27 the Bible says, "It is appointed unto man once to die but after this the judgment."

This life is not the end. No, after we die, we will live forever in one place or another, either heaven or hell.

That is why I thank God for the death of sin. Jesus died on the cross for me; He paid my sin penalty for me through His death on the cross. The power of sin was broken over my life, and God's free gift of salvation became mine at the age of eight. There was nothing I did or could have done to deserve this gift. I simply chose to make it mine. This was truly a glorious death and a glorious resurrection to new life in Christ.

If you have experienced the death of sin in your life, be sure to tell others, for God is not willing that any should perish.

"The Lord is not slack concerning his promise, as some men count slackness; but is longsuffering to us-ward, not willing that any should perish, but that all should come to repentance" (2 Peter 3:9).

My song as an eight-year-old girl in Massillon, Ohio was "Into my heart, into my heart, Come into my heart, Lord Jesus. Come in today. Come in to stay, come into my heart Lord Jesus." And He did! Here are a few verses from the "Untitled Hymn" by Chris Rice showing the progress we go through as a new Christian. It is important to remember that we start off as a new born baby in Christ and then we grow through His Word just like a child would grow.

Weak and wounded sinner
Lost and left to die
O, raise your head, for love is passing by
Come to Jesus and live!

Now your burden's lifted
And carried far away
And precious blood has washed away the stain, so
Sing to Jesus and live!

And like a newborn baby
Don't be afraid to crawl
And remember when we walk
Sometimes, we fall
Fall on Jesus and live!

Chapter 2

The Death of Purity

We now move to my junior high school journey. These days were filled with church camps, football games (I am from Massillon, Ohio the birthplace of football, after all), dances, friendships, parties, and, of course, many church activities.

At the age of twelve, I went forward at my church and surrendered my life to full-time Christian service. I know that every Christian is in full-time service; what I mean is I knew then that my profession and life would be devoted primarily to His service. This had been one of the desires of my heart. Mrs. Carl Murphy, one of my middle school Sunday school class teachers, asked my class to write down what we thought we would be doing ten years in the future, place the note in an envelope, and address it to our parents. Mrs. Murphy then kept those notes, and after ten years had passed, she mailed them out to our parents. My parents forwarded my letter on to me. It read that I was married to a young pastor, and we were involved with youth and pastoring. I also wrote that my "Pastor husband

and I also sing together." Well, lo and behold, all of this came to pass. I wish I still had that letter to share with you, but it was accidentally thrown away, which made me very sad. It will, however, be forever in my mind.

I believe that this was the time in my life when I came to the cross for surrender, to claim Jesus as Lord of my life. I knew that I wanted to be used of God and wanted to be surrendered to Him and whatever He had for my life.

It was at this stage of my life, in seventh grade, that my path sharply turned down the valley of a dark death. That year, someone I should have been able to look up to and trust, one of my teachers, took advantage of me. I was very naïve, and just like many girls at that age, I fell for the flattery of this man. He told me how pretty, smart, and special I was. He paid extra attention to me. I was certainly the teacher's pet. He built me up to my parents and told me grades that I had earned before other students knew their grades. He became my summer school teacher also, and I sat right in front of his desk.

One time, he asked me to babysit for his children. He and his wife had different appointments and had driven separate cars. On that night, he came home first. His children were asleep, and while waiting for his wife to arrive so he could drive me home, he lured me into a room where he had me sit on his lap and told me what a lovely and special girl I was to him. He then did things that I knew were wrong, and I felt trapped. It is hard now to believe that I did not run out of the house and over to a neighbor's screaming, but this happened in the early '60s. I had never heard of this happening to anyone, and it was nighttime.

I was so taken back that I believe I was in shock. At night I would lay in bed and rehearse the details in my mind. Shame and sadness filled me from the inside out. How did this happen to someone who loves Jesus so much? What could I have done? Where was God? Why did I allow this to happen? Why was I afraid to speak out? I do not have the answers to those questions except to say, God knows. I never ever in my life would have thought that would happen to me. Even now as I pen these words my whole being is in pain with the memories this brings back to mind.

I wish I could tell you that the one time it happened was the end, and physically, it did end. I never babysat for his children again, but emotionally, it continued. I was very drawn to this teacher for the accolades he poured onto me, feeding my need for acceptance and approval. He would drive by my house and honk the horn on his car and wave, doing just enough little things to keep me under his controlling power and, in reality, bound in shame-based thinking. I was too ashamed to speak out both for his actions and my response. This continued until I left middle school for high school. All the while, I kept up a front of being spiritual; I'm sorry to say. It is easy to live both sides of the fence. I am so sorry.

I never told my parents as I could not hurt them in this way, even though I was the one who was taken advantage of. Besides, I knew if I told my parents they would have really gone after him. Seriously, my parents would have protected me. Now, years later, I wish I would have told them so this man would have been exposed for the pervert that he was. He probably hurt others besides myself.

I did not even tell my husband until much later in our marriage. I cannot tell you the profound impact this had on my life. I was crippled by this traumatic experience for many years, and it was not until a few years ago, around '93, that I came to grips with this.

I heard a radio program that talked about sexual abuse, and instead of stuffing it down deep inside, I thought, *Oh my goodness, that happened to me!* I then began to deal with all the hurt and pain it had caused me over all those years.

I did not realize it, but I had a lot of built-up anger inside me from this and knew that I never wanted anyone to experience this type of awful attack. Healing takes time.

When I started dealing with the trauma of my past and sought council, the counselor wanted me to share this story with my family so they could understand some of my actions (the anger and fears I had), so I did.

In reality, I was not ready to do so. I felt very ashamed, and I did not feel my younger children could understand what I was saying. I just pray that God used my brokenness.

If you have been through a death of purity through no fault of your own, there is healing. In God's time, you will be able to share how God has healed you. First, you must acknowledge the brokenness.

Growing up, I respected authority, and I thought that meant never disappointing anyone. I respected authority over me and had the mindset that if anyone was wrong, it was me. Performance-based acceptance was a huge part of my life. I believed that if I did everything right, I would be perfectly loved and accepted. Funny, but I know my parents loved and accepted me; they did not consciously teach this to me. My mother especially was very active at church, and we went to church together as a family every time the doors were open. Being the last child at home, often I had to go to the adult meetings during the week with Mom and Dad because they did not want to leave me, so I had a lot of adult interaction.

But, I also remember having to sing, without fail, a song for others before we left an event. Sometimes I did not feel like singing, but I did, and it needed to be right. As I look back now, I know my parents just wanted me to share my talent, and they challenged me. I am grateful for that now; I'm just telling you the effect it had on me then. One time I messed up at a dance recital, and I knew Mother was upset with me. I knew I would be punished. Upon arrival home, Mother proceeded to tear my dance costume off me—all the pretty sequins and buttons went everywhere. When I told my husband about this experience after many years of marriage, he said, "I bet you were really mad at your mom."

"No," I said. "I was instead so sad that I had failed my mother by messing up in the recital."

He could not believe it, but it was true. Please know by sharing this event, I mean no disrespect to my mother. She was sweet, kind, and loving; she only wanted me to grow and learn, and I know that. She reacted in the only way she knew how at the time.

Dance recital

One time, she was trying to teach me measurements, how many feet were in a yard and so forth, as we were driving home from our grocery store. She was quizzing me, and, well, I never have been good at math, so I stumbled at the answers. She told me that I had better give her the right answers by the time we got home, or she would take a yardstick and put the answer across my bottom. Well now, that made me remember quick!

Performance-based acceptance is a learned behavior that I was taught early. This behavior transferred to the abuse I endured by my teacher. I did not want to fail him. How warped is that? I, of course, could not tell anyone what had happened. I was so ashamed, so humiliated. My parents could not know, so they both went to their graves not knowing about his abuse of me. His abuse of me happened long before it was okay to speak out about this type of thing. Looking back, I would love to expose that teacher (who is probably dead by now) for what he really was and have him be punished. I was a minor. I know in my heart, I was not his only victim. Even though the physical abuse was one time only, the emotional, flirting, abuse continued holding me hostage in my own mind.

Isn't is crazy how sin is? What I knew was horribly wrong and hurtful was not easy to end. Someone I looked up to thought I was pretty, special, and even though it was wrong, it was flattering, I guess it goes back to Genesis 3 and the tree of the knowledge of good and evil. Doing what is wrong always seems more exciting, and doing it puts us in control, not God. I believe as I entered high school, I was ready to give up the childish control the teacher had over my life and start fresh. I know my faith is what held me together during those years, even if I did not put it all into practice. God was protecting me, and His Hand was on my life.

Many years later, my husband and I drove up to my hometown and sat in our car outside this teacher's house (he still lived there), where I poured out my heart of all the pain, shame, and agony he caused me throughout all these years. It seems crazy, but toward the end of my outpouring, the curtains parted inside his house, and there he was, looking out to see who was in front of his house! Of course, he would not recognize me now. However, this did give me an opportunity to come face to face with him from the car. I said, "Yes, Mr.___, I forgive you." After a time, symbolically, I opened my car door and let all the dirt and drama of that time in my life flow out onto the curb in front of his house. It felt good to finally deal with this. A huge burden was lifted off me as we drove away that day. This death to me was a very sad death. It was one of the major events that caused me to be a shame-filled person. I had carried this with me for so long... but I found resurrection power through forgiveness.

If you have dealt with this kind of death in your life, there is relief. One of the books that really helped me the most after I came to grips with all of this was titled *Released from Shame* by Sandra D. Wilson. This book was very difficult for me to read, and I had to put it down many times and come back to it when I was ready to begin again. Also, doing something dramatic, like I did when we drove up to the teacher's house, is helpful. Another way to express your hurt and get rid of it is to write a letter to the person who hurt you. Let your feelings all come out in writing. Then, put the letter in an envelope and with a big red marker write "Forgiven for Jesus's sake." Now, take the letter and burn it, or bury it deep somewhere where you will never see it again, and the person never sees the letter. All of these activities help to bring peace.

My life continued into high school with voice lessons with Irene Beamer, parts in school musicals under the direction of Byron Griest, singing with groups and singing solos all over town... It was my honor to sing a solo at my high school baccalaureate service. I received the highest music award that our high school gave, the Arian award which thrilled my heart, and interestingly enough, the award was presented to me by a wonderful pastor in the area.

Finally, my school years were coming to a close, and it was time to think about college.

Singing at my High School Baccalaureate Service.

High School graudation 1966 Washington High School, Massillon, Ohio

Chapter 3

The Death of Personality

Because of my parents' work schedules, we really did not visit colleges. I basically applied to the schools I was interested in for my major. I wanted to pursue Christian education and music.

My mother knew three schools that were good choices for me. One of them was Wheaton College in Illinois, another Malone College in Canton (close to home), and the last one was Bob Jones University in Greenville, South Carolina. We completed and mailed in my applications and tests scores to all three schools. Mother said whichever school I was accepted into first would be where we would trust I was to attend. Bob Jones University was the first to respond, so I left for Greenville, South Carolina the fall following high school graduation. Until the day I walked onto campus, I knew nothing about this university.

It was beautiful, but I did not feel ready to be away from home. My parents stuck around for almost a week, and I stayed with them most of the daytime hours. At night, I would go to my dorm room to get acquainted with my three roommates. Finally, I said a painful goodbye to my parents and started full-time life in the dorm. My roommates were so incredible, especially during my freshman year, as Carolyn and Dorothy took me under their wings to help me adjust to college life. Later on, one of my roommates, Shirley, was a bridesmaid in my wedding.

Bob Jones University (BJU) was a very strict school (especially in the '70s). I really did not mind, as I was brought up to respect rules. After all, I was there for an education. I only received one demerit in the four years I was there—for being too loud on Friday night. BJU had quiet hours from seven until ten in the evening *on Fridays*! Hey, I am from the football town of Massillon, and our games were on Friday nights. Fridays were *never* quiet back home.

While I was growing up, I was always a free spirit, so the one thing that happened to me during my college years was going down the valley of the shadow of the death of my personality. Do you think that is strange? Yes, it is! The strangest thing about it, as I look back now, is that I caused this shadow of death of my personality to come over me! You see, I respected all the rules and regulations and did not try to rebel against them, but the rules and such stifled me. I believe it was because I had a free lifestyle in high school. On my own, I stifled myself. Gone was the carefree Joy who enjoyed Friday night football games. Instead, I began to think more highly of myself and look down on others who were not as 'spiritual" as me. Oh, my! Perhaps it was performance-based acceptance rearing its ugly head again. I did not want to fail, so I needed to, on my own, dot every "i" and cross every "t." I was

20

afraid to be free again and became more subdued. There is nothing wrong with being spiritual and sub-dued, but it is wrong when taken to an extreme. This death of personality caused me to be more fearful of possible failure, more inward, more critical. It was a death I brought on myself; it was totally unnecessary. I'm so glad God showed me this, and I could learn from the experience.

Don't get me wrong; I love BJU. I received a won-derful education there that I would not trade. I am thankful and proud of my education there. My BJU leaders and teachers were wonderful to me. Not all students experienced what I did, but some did. I was not ruined by any means but just not the person I really was down deep inside.

Graduation from BJU. Bob & Me with my parents

Graduation arrived, and I was privileged to give a testimony during commencement on one of Dr. Bob Jones Sr.'s sayings. I chose, "A man may be saved in an instant, but it takes a life time to develop Christian character." I have found this saying true in my life. I was saved at the age of eight, and yet, I am still growing, learning, and maturing in Christ. So many of Dr. Bob Sr.'s sayings have stayed with me through all these years.

The university has changed so much over the years. Not in their Biblical stand, but in some of their strict ways, which is good. I still highly respect all of the Dr. Bobs, especially Dr. Bob III, and would recommend the education. I used to care for Bob Jones IV when I worked in the university's nursery.

If you have ever found yourself in a time period that caused a death in your personality, there is healing also. If your change was like mine, and you were stifled from being who you really are, you may ask God to restore to you the joy of your life and to help you be a blessing to others. His word says so. Psalm 51:12-13 reads, "Restore unto me the joy of thy salvation; and uphold me with thy free spirit. Then will I teach transgressors thy ways; and sinners shall be converted unto thee."

Perhaps you are just the opposite of me. Perhaps God wants to use you, but you are holding back because of not yielding to all He wants you to be. He can free you to be open to others and use you for His glory; just ask Him. "You have not, because ye ask not. Ye ask, and receive not, because ye ask amiss, that ye may consume it upon your lusts" (James 4:2-3).

God made you just the way you are, and He is able to use you in His service to reach others. He will use you in ways that He does not use me. You will be able to reach people that I am not able to reach. That is the beauty of God's creation.

We are to be a testimony of God's love in our life, not be bound by a set of rules and regulations to try and change others. Christ died to set us free from that and to give us an abundant life of peace and joy in Him. Yes, we follow His guidelines, but we do it because we are loved and accepted by Him, not to attain His love and acceptance.

The death of personality for a time was a very troublesome death for me and I am so thankful for healing and a restored life to my true personality. God loves to restore. My life verse is Psalm 104:33: "I will sing unto the LORD as long as I live: I will sing praise to my God while I have my being."

Do you have a life verse? If not, claim one today. Ask God to lead you to just the right verse, and He will!

There is resurrection through acceptance. Not our acceptance of Christ this time but knowing that God accepts us perfectly. Right here, I want to say that there is relief from performance-based acceptance. When you realize who you are in Christ (for example accepted in the Beloved) and how much you matter to God, you don't have to prove your worth to the world. "To the praise of the glory of his grace, wherein he hath made us accepted in the beloved" (Ephesians 1:6). We too often dwell on our circumstances (our condition) in life, and this will not change our hearts. Meditate instead on your position, who you are in Christ according to Scripture, and watch your life change! Your condition is always changing, but your position in Christ will never change.

My education continued with the joy of the Lord.

Meeting Bob

Meeting Bob at BJU was a huge blessing to me. We met during the second semester of our freshman year 1967 in Radio Choir.

Yes, it was a choir that recorded and sang for radio programs. Bob was already in the choir, and I joined my second semester. I remember there were five of us new girls that semester and as we all walked into the room that day, Bob looked at all of us and said, "Hi, girls, my name is Bob."

Oh, you big flirt, I thought. *I am going to get you!*

Once, while Bob and I were standing in front of the snack shop, I asked him if he had ever sung a duet with anyone. "We could make beautiful music together," he replied. His comment was interesting, because I thought so too, though I laughed. On one of our first performances together, the two of us sang a duet in front of the student body. We really liked each other, and our feelings continued to grow stronger, but we did no want to rush anything. We decided we would "loke" each other for a while because that was halfway between like and love.

Because guys and girls were not allowed to talk after going to your dorm after supper, we continued to write notes to each other, which were delivered to the dorms every night at ten o'clock, just after quiet hours. These notes were pushed underneath dormitory room doors. Ours were always signed "With all my Loke." Then, April 25, 1967, while Bob was walking me down what was called the "date line" (the path a guy took to walk a girl back to her dorm after supper), Bob told me that the "k" in "loke" had turned to a "v."

He loved me! I told him that I loved him too and floated up to my dorm room that evening.

April 25 became our love day, which we celebrate every year.

We were engaged on our way back to BJU after Christmas break, on January 3, 1968. We had gone to Paris Mountain in South Carolina. Bob had driven from California to pick me up in Massillon, so we could travel back to BJU together. (My brother used to say that Bob was the only person he knew that had the United States as his neighborhood!)

Bob had always told me he would not ask me to marry him until he had an engagement ring. He worked so hard to pay for a ring; then, he had an auto accident over Christmas break on his way from Ohio to California, which took all his savings.

He used to tease me while walking down the date line after super by telling me that he had something in his pocket. I would get all excited thinking it was the ring. "What...?" I would ask.

"Oh, I have some old gum wrappers, toothpicks..." Sometimes he would say "I have something I want to ask you..."

Of course I thought he was going to pop the marriage question, but instead, he would say, "Would you... would you be my pal?" Oh, my!

So, at Paris Mountain, Bob is stumbling around, and he sits me down on a bench, gets down on one knee, and begins to ask me a question while reaching for his back pocket.

Knowing he had to spend up all of his savings to fix his car, after he was done with his little speech and started to say,"Will you..."(But he hadn't shown me a ring), I proceeded to pat him on the head and said, "Yes, I will be your pal."

"NO, I am serious!" he said. I almost fell off the bench! After I got my composure, I said "YES!!"

Engagment at Paris Moutain

He very carefully placed a ring on my finger, and it was stunning. We still had about three hours before we were expected to return to campus, and if you know anything about Bob Jones University, that was a big deal.

Well, I was so excited about the engagement that I asked him to take me back to my dorm right away. I wanted to tell everyone and show them my ring. Poor Bob, he drove me back and later said I did not even wait for the car door to close before running up three flights of stairs to say to everyone, "Look what I just got!"

That evening, we met before supper at the dining hall before going to our separate assigned tables, and we said "Hi" to each other. I just have to laugh, what a romance we had at BJU! God allowed us to really get to know and appreciate one other. Bob was from California, and I was from Ohio; it was truly a God thing!

Over Christmas break of my senior year at BJU, I married the love of my life. We were married on December 21, 1969. We then became town students and graduated together in May of 1970.

Wedding

Chapter 4

The Death of Plans

From Florida to Ohio to Kansas and Back to Ohio Again

After college graduation in 1970, we moved to Milton, Florida, and both taught in a wonderful Christian school there. I taught third grade, and Bob taught fourth. We knew we were only going to be there for a year, as God wanted us in church youth ministry. That is where our heart was focused. We, however, thought it would be good to be out in the public teaching for one year as we felt so young. It seems funny now to even think about being so young.

I was so excited to live in Florida (even though we lived in the panhandle, near Pensacola, so it was almost Alabama) because my brother and his wife lived in the same state. Bob and I decided that we would visit them over Thanksgiving break.

Well, they lived in Miami, and we were near Pensacola, so we spent the majority of our time driving to their home. We arrived, sat down and had a delicious Thanksgiving meal, and then we had to head right back to Milton. But it was great to be with family.

Now, let me share with you an example of legalism and why my husband and I have been cured of it. The school we taught in was a great place to work, but it was very legalistic. Legalism is a set of rules and reg-ulations set to make you "seem" more spiritual. I like to do what is right because of Who Christ is not to prove to someone that I am spiritual. The church for the school was the school, which is fine, I understand that for a time. The school was fairly new so it takes time to expand to have a separate church building. So, Sunday church met in the cafeteria—where we ate lunch with our students through the week. Because all the leadership positions in the church were filled, to have a place to serve, Bob and I had joined the choir and sang in it every Sunday. When we returned from our Miami visit, we learned that we had been kicked out of the choir because we missed a rehearsal they had over Thanksgiving break. We told them we would be gone, but it made no difference. So, for the rest of the year that we taught there, we had no openings for service in the church. No matter how you look at this, it was wrong. With legalism showing up, and in our first job position, we were cured of legalism having experienced it through the years in other situations. Now, the opposite of legalism is license. License to do, say, act, or think however you want. I do not believe in either concept.

We still gave our all to the school and teaching, then God opened a door for us to fly to Wichita, Kansas, to candidate at a wonderful church out there for its youth minister position. Bob knew the pastor there because of connections back at Bob's home church in California.

Position in Kansas Fell through: 1971

We were so excited and spent a wonderful weekend in Kansas. The pastor told us that all was in order for us to be accepted as the new youth pastor, and he would send us a letter to confirm this decision. We went back to Florida and resigned our teaching positions effective at the end of the school year. After about a month, the letter came from Pastor Doyle Hopper of Bible Baptist in Wichita, Kansas. It was a very painful letter to read. The youth pastor who had planned to leave had decided to stay, and there was no open position for us. Our hearts and plans were devastated.

It was a painful road down the valley of the shadow of death of plans for us. We did candidate at a couple of Florida churches, but nothing worked out. In our particular denomination, when we desire to take a position at a church, we say we go to candidate for that position. In other words, we go and basically do all that position requires as leadership observes us. We are also asked many questions about our standards and beliefs—to see if we would be a good "fit" for the church. It is like interviewing for a job. When we candidated, we looked at each position separately. We did not want to compare positions for the wrong reasons. We wanted to be where God wanted us to be. (Someone had given us this advice, and it is right, so I pass it on in case you ever find yourself in this situation.)

Moved in with Parents in Ohio: 1971

At the end of the school year, we rented a small U-Haul trailer and headed off to Massillon, Ohio. We moved into the basement of my parents' home. Bob went to work as one of the custodians for Canton Baptist Temple, and I worked alongside my mother at the nursing home on the dementia wing. She was the head nurse there. We were humbled and somewhat confused, but God used those jobs in our life to grow us. God had to put us in these areas to keep us relying on Him and not pushing our agenda. God knows what is best. We also did a lot of speaking and singing at different churches including Canton Baptist Temple which was my home church and at some of the camps at Camp CHOF (Christian Hall Of Fame).

Our Plywood Paradise: 1971

While Bob was speaking at a junior camp at Camp CHOF, Pastor Al Barbie from New Philadelphia, Ohio came and talked to him about working together at his church, First Baptist Church of New Philadelphia, Ohio. After about a month, we were in full-time service there as youth, music, and associate pastor. We moved from my parents' home to what we called our little "plywood paradise." (I thought it was all paneling, but Bob told me it was plywood) on Union Avenue in Dover, Ohio.

On a side note, if you are like me and get upset when you hear the complaints and pickiness of people who want everything perfect in a house while watching some of the house hunter shows on TV, you can be sure that most likely no one would have wanted our plywood paradise. But we were happy as could be. I am thankful for that, and I believe it goes back to my upbringing, where we were taught the biblical principle of being content with and in whatever you have. We had a wonderful ministry in New Philadelphia; we served with wonderful people, but after a year, the lead pastor took another position and moved away. They offered the church to Bob (a church on the move with great potential ahead), but Bob had been called to youth work and did not feel called at that time to be a senior pastor.

To this day, I am blessed by the year we had in New Philadelphia—the lives that were touched there, and the friendships that remain.

Kansas Job Opened Up: 1972

We then (all in God's timing) received a call from Pastor Hopper in Wichita, Kansas. He called to tell us that the youth pastor position was now open, and he wanted us to come and be a part of the staff there. It was 1972, and we served there until early 1976. We rented another U-Haul and were on our way to Kansas. The youth ministry that we had candidated for was not the same as what we moved into. The ministry had gone down, and we were challenged to build it up again. By God's grace, it became one of the largest and most productive youth ministries of the Midwest. All glory to God.

So, you see, our plans are not always His plans or His timing. We learn to be submissive to Him. He is always working His good into our life, so we must trust Him.

God gave us a most incredible ministry there and blessed us beyond measure. So many of the youth are now in ministry or faithfully serving the Lord. The impact of those years in Kansas will never be known until eternity. Of course, that is the case wherever God gives you the opportunity of serving for Him.

No Children and Possible Move

While we were in Wichita, I experienced a deep valley of the shadow of the death of plans. At the time, I thought this one was the most devastating death.

Bob and I were blessed by the ministry in Kansas, and we thought we would be there the rest of our life. We then proceeded to make plans to start a family.

After long trials of testing, medications, and surgery, we discovered I could not bear children. Being in youth work did not make this knowledge easier to bear. One of our top leaders in the youth group became pregnant out of wedlock. Forgive me, but I could hardly contain myself. Here we were in ministry and could not have children, and this unmarried couple who were so promising for ministry were expecting! I am ashamed of my response now, but this was back in the 70s. "Why Lord?" I asked. "Why? Bob and I are trying to be faithful to You, and we are not able to bear children."

I must include that the couple went on to be married and the husband and the baby have been greatly used by God; I am so thankful for that. Finally, after my pity party and heartbreak, we became excited about the possibility of adopting a child. There was never any hesitation in our mind about adopting.

My heart loves women who will give their babies to adoptive parents instead of having an abortion. We do not know all the circumstances for not being able to care for a baby or child, but we do know abortion is not the answer. We also know that many couples want to adopt a baby or child. We were delighted to get on a waiting list and were very excited about what God was going to do for us.

After some months, the Lord began to deal with us about becoming a senior pastor and taking a church somewhere. We had what we called a "holy restlessness in our heart." Then, the Lord began to produce a desire in us to love an entire church through our leadership. We felt we had so much to share through Bob's preaching and the principles of the cross that God had been teaching us. The Lord had also provided wonderful opportunities for us to work with seasoned missionaries and make an impact on their lives through what He was teaching us. We just had to expand. This was different for us, and we were apprehensive but excited about the possibilities. *Maybe it will be a big church, and we will get to have movers instead of a U-Haul!* I wondered. We began to wait for God's leading.

As time went by, it became abundantly clear that God was not going to send us to an already established church, but He was calling on us to start a church. Ohio started to come more and more into the forefront, and before we knew it, we were packing up a U-Haul trailer with all our earthly goods and heading toward Westerville, Ohio to begin a church. The name that God had given us for the church was Calvary (because of the impact of the cross on our life) Bible (because we wanted the Word of God to be central in our baby church) Baptist: Calvary Bible Baptist.

On March 12, 1976, we arrived in Westerville. Everything had fallen into place for our move, except all the time we had accrued on the adoption list in Wichita. We lost it because it was not transferable to another state. *Lord, what are you doing*? we wondered. This was a desire of our heart, and we were delighting in Him.

Church Born and Hopes for a Family: 1976

Before we actually started the church, I saw an ad for a woman's luncheon in the city and thought I would attend. I did not know anyone, so I was not sure where to sit. I randomly chose a seat and began talking to a lady at the table. She asked the typical questions when you are getting acquainted including the one: "Do you have any children?" I explained to her that we did not have children but were wanting to adopt. I told her how, upon arrival here in Ohio, we had gone around to all the adoption agencies, but none of them were open to infant adoption. She looked at me and said, 'We have an attorney in our church who specializes in adoptions, let me give you his name." I then breathed a prayer, "Lord, thank You for directing me to the exact seat I should sit in today." You really may trust God to do those "little things" in your life. (It was a very big issue for us.)

My Husband and I immediately contacted the attorney and scheduled an appointment. We were then placed for some time on his waiting list.

Our first service at Calvary Bible Baptist was April 25, 1976. It was the anniversary of our "love day." We refer to the starting of the church as our "labor of love."

It's a Boy: 1978

Always dreamed of being a Mommy

Amazingly, after a time, we were matched with a baby who was expected to be born on May 10, 1978. On that date exactly, we were excited to hear the news that we were the parents of a baby boy.

My parents had moved from Massillon to Westerville to be near us for the church ministry. They, of course, wanted to be at our home when the attorney brought our new baby boy to the house for us. He arrived straight from the hospital. Well, my husband decided that it would be only him and me at the house that day. This did not sit well with my parents or with all the church people who also wanted to be there. However, everyone honored our wish.

Well, after the attorney delivered Timothy Paul Burney to our door, we unwrapped the blankets and were amazed by our son! The Bible verse that came to my mind was Ephesians 3:20 : "Now unto Him who is able to do exceeding, abundantly above all that we ask or think, according to the power that worketh in us." This then became Tim's verse. He was more wonderful than we could ever have imagined, and we have claimed this verse and prayed it for him all through his life, not knowing when we unwrapped that blanket what all his life would face.

After we checked out all his little fingers and toes, Bob said, "Call your parents; call everyone and tell them to get over here and see our baby!" We did just that! What an incredible blessing to us!

"How sweet to hold our newborn baby and feel the pride and joy he gives. But greater still the calm assurance this child can face uncertain days because Christ lives." We just felt like these lyrics from *Because He Lives* by the Gaithers.

Second Adoption Falls through: 1983

When our son was around four years old, we were presented with an opportunity to adopt an eighteen-month-old baby girl. Once again, we were excited and moved Timothy over to a bigger room, so we could turn his former room back into a nursery. We planned to name her Melody Joy. On the day she was expected to arrive at our home, the three of us—me, Bob, and Timothy—were watching out our living room window awaiting her arrival. Then the phone rang. Our attorney said something had come up in the hearing; the birth father needed to give permission for the adoption...it should just be a matter of days...they had to find him. Days turned into weeks and weeks into months.

Finally, permission was given, so the adoption was a go. A couple days later, the attorney called and told us that the birth mother had changed her mind and would be keeping the baby. Well, that was okay for that Mother, we were happy for her, but we were devastated. It was another valley of the shadow of death of plans for us. I think maybe this is what a miscarriage must feel like. You are expecting a little one, then that expectation is taken away. Our little world fell in. All three of us were disappointed. Walking past that once again nursery room was like walking by a morgue. It was awhile before we changed the room back.

The Mighty, Mighty Burneys: 1984

The 3 children

Then, five years after the Lord blessed us with Tim, we received a phone call from a friend who knew we wanted to adopt more children. The voice on the other end asked me if we would be interested in adopting twins. She knew of twin girls who were going to be given over to Children's services that very day by their birth mother. I immediately called Bob at the church office and told him. Bob said to give the name of our attorney to this lady, so she could give it to her friend. If her friend decided to cancel her Children's Services appointment that day and contact our attorney, well, we would just trust God to put this all together according to His will, but we would stay out of it. I did just that, and twenty-one days later, in February of 1984, those twin girls came through our door calling us Mommy and Daddy and their brother "Tennessee" because they could not say Timothy! We were now a family of five! The girls were not identical, but I could not tell them apart. I remember I used to sit up in bed at night making a list of their characteristics. One of them wore glasses, but when they were not facing forward, I did not know! The verse that God gave us for the girls was Leviticus 20:26 which reads: "And ye shall be holy unto me: for I the LORD *am* holy, and have severed you from *other* people, that ye should be mine." And we have claimed this for both of them.

Did I mention that the twin girls were five years old? They were the same age as Timothy. Now, we were the parents of three five year olds who were only a month apart. Tim's birthday is May 1978 and the girls were born in June that same year.

It was interesting when someone asked how old our children were. (And it still is.) I would share that they were all the same age but remark that the three were not triplets. They all three looked so much alike. When God puts a family together, He does it right! I remember going on vacation shortly after the adoption and a lady saying to me, "Oh, honey, you had your family all at once, didn't you?" I just nodded my head yes. God made us a family, and God does all things well. As I write this book, they are all approaching forty.

All three of our children were dedicated to the Lord. We love them all so very much. The adoption of all our children was totally from God. It is a miracle story. We have always said that we are a miracle family. I remember the very first night with all three children at home. Everyone was so hyper. Bob took all three of them downstairs to the family room, while I unpacked the girls' things. As I sat on the floor in the girls' room, I remember looking up toward heaven saying, "Lord, I pray someone is praying for me right now because I really need it!" I was overwhelmed by the task that was before us. An infant is easier to adopt because you immediately have a bond, but we were positive this was God's will for our life, and we already had love in our heart for the twins.

Our girls came to us from their birth mother. They had lived with others at different times, so they were very independent. They were learning to print their names, so we did not change them. We did, however, begin to tell them that we wanted to give them a gift. That gift was our last name. We wanted them to become Burneys. At our interlocutory hearing to finalize the girls' adoption, we asked the judge to pound the gavel and pronounce us Burneys. She did so with great gusto. As soon as she did, the five of us joined hands and sang to the judge. "We are the Burneys, the mighty, mighty Burneys. Everywhere we go, people want to know, who we are, so we tell them. We are the Burneys!"

Just as we exited the room, there was a power failure in downtown Columbus. All the lights were out and elevators were not working. The children were all afraid. So, we continued to hold hands and lead all the children down eighteen flights of stairs. Of course, we were still singing "we are the Burneys" which echoed all through the court house. God is so good.

Through the Years

Our Burney Family

As a family of five, we have shared numerous laughs, shed tears, and we have experienced good and bad times and everything in-between. I firmly believe that God gave me the children He blessed me with for one main reason (among others). I believe God placed them in our home that I (we) might intercede for them. Intercession is a huge blessing to do for each of our children. I take them individually before the Lord and present their needs and longings. If God will use me to intercede on their behalf, then I will be the most blessed mother ever. I have spent these past thirty-nine plus years interceding through prayer for them, and I have no intention of quitting. I have seen God do the miraculous in their lives; I know God has heard my prayers for them. I have seen physical healing, emotional healing, and relational healing. I have seen God perform miracles. I have also watched as dreams crumbled before me, and I have seen devastation, but all the while, I remain confident that God will use all for His Glory. The most important part of life is God's glory, and He alone knows what to do for that. We may petition God for what we think is best, but the final decision is His. My parents interceded for me and my heart is so thankful for their prayers. Prayer is powerful, and I am a believer that God does nothing but by prayer. I love the song *What a Friend We Have in Jesus* by Joseph M. Scriven which says, "Oh what peace we often forfeit, oh what needless pain we bear. All because we do not carry everything to God in prayer."

I do know that prayer brings peace. If you do not have peace about a situation, keep on praying until peace comes. Adopted children have unique needs, and guess what, so do adoptive parents.

I finally broke down one day, many years after our children arrived, and shared with Bob the physical loss I felt. Not knowing what a child that we biologically produced would look like: Would her or his hair be curly? Would he or she love to sing? Would he follow in his dad's footsteps someday and be a preacher? Would she want to be like me? Oh, I had so many questions. How does it feel for your baby to kick in your tummy? How is it to have your husband put his hand on your stomach and feel the baby kicking? How is it to have the ultrasound to find out if the baby is a boy or girl or to wait in the delivery room with your husband at your side and be surprised at the sex of your child as you experience birth?

Now I know that those of you who have given birth would tell me that it is not all that great, but I don't know that. I wept, and Bob held me. But it was okay because we had been incredibly blessed by God with these three children. I would not trade what God gave to us for the world. It was only a fleeting moment, like probably adopted children have too, and it's okay. Feelings, looks and professions mean nothing when you see what God puts together and God had made us a family! We give Him thanks.

May I Introduce My Children

Tim is my hard worker. He is extremely creative, athletic, very knowledgeable, writer of poetry, loves to learn, and a wonderful father to four of our grandchildren. He is a fitness guru with the biggest heart ever. He also is a master griller, has an eye for quality, and things that are lovely. He thrills my heart as he tells me he loves me, appreciates me, and compliments me. We are very close and are able to talk about life together.

Amy (in the white dress) is my book lover. I always loved how she treasured her books through the years. She is a talented artist with a kind heart. She's a real giver to others. Amy is such a loyal worker. She has become a great cook, decorator, and encourager to me. I love that she makes time to get together with me even with her busy schedule. Amy has much knowledge of so many things. We also are very close.

Angela(in the navy dress) was our talented flute player. I say "was" as she no longer plays. I wish she did as she was very good. She is a very social person who loves to cook and decorate. I always appreciated the way she kept her room. She is a busy mother to four of our grandchildren.

Loss, Just Not Enough?

Having one of our twins become very bitter, take her family (four of our grandchildren), and walk away from our family has broken our heart. We are praying it is only for a season, but it has been so long. Satan and our flesh are so powerful, and we live in a world where everything is someone else's fault.

I feel like the family of five that God put all together on February 21 of 1984 has been stepped on. God made us a family; it was His choice. It was and is truly another valley of the shadow of death, the death of family, and we are still praying now for restoration. We are not sure of all the whys and whats. Yes, like other families we went through rough times and illnesses. I take full responsibility for so much of the hurt and pain I must have caused my children because of my fears and anger along with my physical and emotional pain. All of this came from my past issues that had not been dealt with and my un-crucified flesh wanting to be in charge.

To my knowledge, all issues have been confessed openly both publicly and privately, forgiveness has been sought, and confessions have been made to all involved. I was convinced that now, after those rough years, we all had a very close relationship with each one. This current separation came up out of the blue after many good years together. I had asked if I could once again sit down and explain some of the presenting issues in my life that might have caused this, and the person said they did not want to hear. I was also told that "sorry" was not enough. All of my efforts were not enough to heal.

Have you ever felt like you were not enough? Chonda Pierce has dealt with this feeling over the past few years, and it has helped me so much. When you feel like you are not enough, or you have had enough, or that a problem is too big remember God is enough; God is big enough. Sometimes in this life, it is just holding on to a faith-filled helplessness. By this I mean, we are not enough, but God is, and we are sometimes helpless but because of Christ, we are never hopeless. Keep the faith, even if it is the size of a grain of mustard seed: "And Jesus said unto them, Because of your unbelief: for verily I say unto you, If ye have faith as a grain of mustard seed, ye shall say unto this mountain, Remove hence to yonder place; and it shall remove; and nothing shall be impossible unto you" (Matthew 17:20-24).

If you are dealing with a separation for whatever reason, I beg you not to hold on and cuddle it until you have all your satisfactory answers. Don't let another day go by that you don't give it up and allow restoration to come. I know it is true that some would rather hold on to the hurt because it satisfies in some strange way their hurt. Life is short, and none of us have the assurance of tomorrow. The Bible says, "If it be possible, as much as lieth in you, live peaceably with all men." (Romans 12:18).

If you try to reconcile, and the other party does not want reconciliation then continue to pray. You cannot make that person forgive and choose to restore the relationship. It has to be their choice. Christ died for all and desires that all men be reconciled to Him, but all are not. We don't know at this time what will take place in our situation, and it makes us exceeding sad, but we trust.

If you are in a situation like ours and are not able to bear children, I understand. I know today there are so many options for those situations. Each has its challenges, but God will give you peace and supply every need. You see, He is a God Who always cares for us, and He will do what is best for you. We must learn to wait and trust.

Our Georgia Grands when they were young

Also, if you have a child who has removed themselves from the family, release them to the Lord and pray, "Thy will be done." God cares more about the entire situation than we can comprehend. They have freewill, and God is the only One Who can change hearts. We all have dreams and aspirations for our children, and sometimes those dreams are crashed to the ground into a million pieces, and we are broken. But God loves to heal broken people and hearts, and He brings beauty from what we feel has been ruined.

I experienced the valley of the shadow of death of my plans many times, but each struggle, whether ministry or family, God used and is using to bring life!

In ministry, we have met so many wonderful people and have young and old in service for Christ all over the world through the churches, camps, and even the school where God placed us in His perfect timing. Now in our family, we not only have children but have been blessed with wonderful grandchildren! I call them my Grands as they have truly made my life Grand! The death of plans that I thought the most devastating God turned around to wonderful blessings.

Our Burney Grands

More about Our Church

When we moved from Wichita in 1976 to begin the church in Westerville, God miraculously provided a house for us, then a building for us to start the church in, then an actual church, and then our own prime property and church building. It was just the two of us, supported by a couple of churches and a few individuals. We canvased the neighborhood and placed ads in the papers.

My husband was a wonderful, faithful pastor and preacher of the Bible. We were able to establish, through the Lord, a solid foundation of truth for the church. As a family, we gave ourselves for the people. The people were always put first. We served the church faithfully for twenty-five years, and we thank God for all that was accomplished there. It is quite a story all by itself. We saw miracle after miracle in so many ways. A miracle is when something takes place that may only be explained by God doing the work. We also experienced some very deep valleys, but God brought us through all of them. Our theme song for the church was *To God be the Glory, Great Things He Has Done.* It was always God's church, not ours. We just happened to be the couple God chose to begin the church, and I believe we led the people to build it on a solid foundation. My husband, as the pastor, taught the people to love and cherish God's word. So many people accepted Christ there; so many people committed to full-time service there; so much was accomplished for missions there. In fact, even before we were self-supporting, we gave out to missions. Our theme was "If you want to keep it, give it away."

In the end, God gave us more than we could ever imagine. Lives were changed for the kingdom there. I am especially thankful that my parents had such a big part in helping us start that church. They drove down from Massillon for the very first service. It was pouring rain, but my dad acted as the usher and had an umbrella to walk the people into the Blendon Grange, which was our first meeting place. My mom very graciously greeted everyone.

A year later, they moved to Westerville to help in the church. Their prayers and help through the years sustained us in this huge undertaking. My mother always gave me a kiss when I was at church. It was her way of saying, "I am with you to support you." After her death, a dear lady in the church named Wanda Drake took over that task. What a blessing that was. Mom always wanted me to be dressed properly as a pastor's wife also. It is the way I was brought up. I wanted to represent my Lord and my husband properly. It is not often that you get to be the founder of something that even when God calls you to move on, you still may drive by the building and be reminded of the work God used you to lay the foundation for, and thank God that the work and impact still goes on.

Many will be in Heaven because of the preaching and teaching of that church. We feel so blessed. So many true friendships continue from that church, and we are encouraged as we hear stories yet today from lives that were touched. The church has changed over the years from what we envisioned, but the truth of God's Word is still preached and taught for which we are thankful. Then, God called us to begin a new ministry. Talk about a change of plans. We just knew we would spend the rest of our life at the church He had called us to found.

CrossPower Ministries: A New Calling: 2001

Now, God is asking us to step out in faith again and begin a new ministry. Bob and I sat in the family room in what I called the problem house after he returned from a missions trip to Kenya. He was in love with Kenya, and I really thought he was going to ask me to move there with him. I did not know how I would get there since I do not fly due to my meniere's disease (inner ear disorder). Instead, God used this trip to deepen his love for the ministry of the cross. Many open doors on that trip gave Bob opportunities to share with others the liberating truth of the cross. Bob's heart was burdened that this should be our main focus, as the message is so very needed. He even put on our hearts and minds the name of the ministry. It was to be called CrossPower Ministries. At the time, we did not know what would be involved in this new ministry but trusted God to fill in the blanks. Never say never to God because that is just about the time He will give you a new challenge! We felt the call to begin this new ministry, but we did not surrender right away. Instead, we wrestled with God in our hearts over the next two years as we were so happy and content at the church. We were seeing our vision for the church being fulfilled. Exciting times of more salvations, baptisms, missions giving, and growth were taking place. Why would we want to leave now? "Lord, what? We do not understand" was our cry. Finally, during a missions Sunday, as a guest minister spoke at our church, Bob and I felt as if it was only God and us there that Sunday. We quietly went forward and knelt at the altar after the message and told God that we would resign the church and begin CrossPower for whatever that meant. It was a huge step. (It was the first time we had not been on a church staff since marriage.) But, surrendering to God is a huge relief. We resigned the church in 2001 and immediately began seeking meetings at various churches to share the message of the cross. God then started to fill in the blanks of the blank contract we signed when we surrendered to start CrossPower.

After we resigned the church to start CrossPower, all in God's plans (not ours), God opened the door for my husband to work full-time at WRFD Radio as their afternoon drive-time host for a live call-in program Mondays through Fridays. The Lord has used the radio ministry to change countless lives and churches all over. Thousands are being reached daily and are learning to "Listen, Think and Discern." I am so proud of the way God is using him in this service. It was a position he did not seek; it was truly given by God.

This job also helps supplement our income as we left the church with no retirement benefits (was never planned for) and no income, not even a car to drive(the car we drove belonged to the church) and yet God supplied all our needs in His way and time. On the weekends, we go out to churches and events with CrossPower on a love offering basis. God has been faithful to meet our every need. We have found that God is many times never early, but He is always on time, regardless of the situation. We may always trust Him, praise His Name. God is using CrossPower Ministries in a powerful way, even worldwide. Bob has taken the teaching of CrossPower to Moldova and Malawi for many years now. We call it evangelism to Christians.

We are finding that most people understand the cross in relationship to salvation but few know what the cross means to living a consistent, victorious life day by day.

God has also opened the door for us to do marriage conferences. Marriages are in trouble all over, and when people will listen and apply the principles of God's word, these conferences can be a blessing from God, and they are a help to many couples.

You see, the message of the cross for salvation is this: Sin had to be paid for, so Christ died on the cross to pay for your sin. He took your place. In other words, He died so you might live. The message of the cross to the Christian is that Christ died to save you also from yourself, so we may say, "I die so that Christ may live both in me and through me." We die to all that is not of God and allow Him to live. It is a message that is foreign to our world today. We live in a world that is all about me, my wants, and my desires.

We now have the teaching of our "CrossPower Weekends" on Dvd with a study guide. These are available for individuals as well as churches and small groups. Contact www.crosspower.net for more information.

More Change of Plans: It's Time to Move

The valley of the shadow of death of plans has also been the case for us over the years as various situations arose that required us to sell our home and move. Then, we found what we called our dream house. It was perfect in every way, and all of us loved it. It was off the beaten track and had a side road that I could walk down that had no traffic at all. I remember one day while walking, I looked up toward heaven and said out loud "I will never sell this house" because it was a dream come true! Like I mentioned before, never say never to God.

Just a short time after that, due to circumstances out of our control, we had to sell our dream house! I was devastated. So many wonderful memories were made there. Well, we found another house to buy (nothing like our dream house), and our dream house sold. Right at closing, a glitch came up in the inspection and our well failed inspection. We had lived there and never had a problem. So, we had to put in a whole new water system. Now, because of that, we had to spend the money for the down payment on the new house we planned to move into.

Our Rented Home and a Battle with Meningitis

We did not know what to do. We had to be out of our dream house in two days. So, I picked up the Westerville News and looked through the houses for rent. There were two available, and one of them was already taken. We went to see the only one that was still listed. When we walked in, it was totally filled with beautiful furniture.

I asked the man who lived there, "When will this house be available?" He said, "When do you need it?"

"In two days!" I replied.

He said, "No problem, I will call a couple of my buddies and have everything out."

"Really? I asked.

"Yes, we are moving to Florida. My wife is already there, so I will join her." Wow, only God can do that. All of this was not in my plan, but God knew. Now, this rental was actually for sale, so we had to be ready for house showings while we lived there, and in a little over three months, we had to find another house to live in because the rental sold.

During this time, I came down with meningitis and was bed bound. Of course, this also was not in my plans.

Purchased a Foreclosure: The Problem House

When our children were nearing thirteen, my husband found a house that was going into foreclosure, and he bid on it. Guess what? We got the house! It just happened to be an ordinary house in Westerville with six bedrooms. Yes, all six on the second floor. The hallway looked like a bowling alley. We had to purchase the house sight unseen. I will never forget the day we finally saw it. It was a total mess. It probably should have been condemned. When we showed the house to our son, Tim, his response was "I'm not living here." So, we gave him the privilege of tearing off old wallpaper and taking a hammer and putting holes in the walls we would have to repair anyway. I remember all of us painting the outside of the house together. We must have looked like the Waltons. Each child had a shutter or door to paint.

People from the church helped us move again, and I sat in the hallway of the house, still very ill, telling everyone which room to put the boxes in. Over the next months, we totally cleaned up this foreclosed house. After several months, it was lovely. It was, however, the worst house we had ever lived in. Bob and I honestly thought it was demon-possessed. We used to walk around the house on the outside and pray. Then, we would go into every room and walk all around and plead the blood of Christ over each room. We had more problems—in our marriage, individually, and with our children—at that house than any other house we had ever lived in. And we lived in this house longer than any other in our married life, until now.

Even though our efforts made the house look beautiful, it was still like a pig, and we knew that because of all the problems we experienced there.

When we started CrossPower Ministries, we decided, after a while, to sell that house and just rent until we knew more of what God wanted to do with this new ministry. When we sold it, we moved to a rental house and were very happy there. Today, that house that we cleaned up once again turned into the worst house on the block, just like when we purchased it as a foreclosure. To me, that just verified the fact that it was like a pig-possessed house. Here is the reason I refer to that house as pig possessed. You may clean a pig up, but it will eventually return to the mud. That is just what this house did. Oh, my prayer is that I will not be like that. I pray that as God cleanses my heart of devilish ways, that I will not return to that and become a muddy mess again. I am so thankful to the Lord for He has always provided a roof over our head, so I am not complaining, just sharing my experiences. Even in this house, God was molding me in ways I did not even know.

We now live in a nice house that God opened for us to move into, but I will not say I will never move from this house. His ways are not my ways, and His plans are not my plans. I just submit to Him. Or I could say, God has His plans laid out for me, and I will continue to trust His divine plans to direct me. Through all these moves, we still continued to keep U-Haul in business! Still all in God's plan for us.

Chapter 5

Death of Precious Loved Ones

My parents meant the world to me. I never allowed a day go by without making contact with one or both of them. What a privilege that was. We were incredibly close. Being the baby of the home meant that many times it was just Mom, Dad and me. I would say that we were the Three Musketeers. My mom was my greatest fan and encourager. She could not carry a tune in a bucket, but she would sing hymn after hymn to the top of her lungs, mouth all the words to the songs when I was singing solos and blessed my heart. We used to get the crazy giggles (at least that is what we called them). Once we started, we could not stop.

My dad was a whistler and a singer and had the biggest smile ever. He called me his "Miss America." His heart was as big as his smile. My father suffered a heart attack before I left for college, so Mother went on to become a nurse to help financially. Both of them were hard workers.

Mom was very involved in church ministry. Both of them ministered not only to me but anyone they came in contact with. Their home was always open. Many times, as I am sure we all do, I thought about the day when one or both of my parents would die. I used to cry just thinking about it.

Mom and Dad Forgan

One day my mom was admitted to the hospital for tests as she had not been feeling well. On the third day there she was to have a heart catheterization. Bob had gone to see her first to read scripture and pray with her. Then, he came home to get me as I was caring for our four-year-old son, Timothy. Bob drove me to the hospital, and I went up to Mom's room to be with her before they took her for the test. She was very restless.

I started to rub her back, and she told me not to do that. She was a nurse, so I believe she knew what might be going on at that time. I assured her that I was there for her. I could see she was in distress. She was lying facing my dad, and there was a window on the other side of the room. Suddenly, she turned toward the window and said, "What?" It was then my mother was escorted to heaven. I called for help, and they tried to save her, but she was already gone. To this day, I believe an angel flew in that hospital window and said, "Beulah Pearl, it's time to go HOME to Jesus." And off they flew.

She had always taught me, from the time I was a little girl, that this world is not our home. When we accept Christ as our Savior, He promised us a home in heaven with Him. There is life after death, and as I mentioned before, you will either spend eternity in heaven or hell depending on what you did with Christ. John 3:16-18 in the Bible says:

> For God so loved the world, that He gave His only begotten Son that whosoever believes in Him should not perish but have everlasting life. For God sent not his Son into the world to condemn the world; but that the world through him might be saved. He that believeth on him is not condemned: but he that believed not is condemned already, because he hath not believed in the name of the only begotten Son of God.

Here I was faced with seeing my mother die and pass into eternity! I was truly in the very presence of the valley of the shadow of death. I remember leaving the hospital and heading home with my dad. We needed gas in our car, so we stopped at a local station. I remember looking out the window and watching people pump gas; I wanted to scream out to them, "Hey, don't you know my mother just died?" *How can the world go on?* I wondered. Well, God promises to give us strength as our days, and He did that for me. "Thy shoes shall be iron and brass; and as thy days, so shall thy strength be" (Deuteronomy 33:25).

Before, just thinking about this possibility made me cry, and now it was a reality. God filled me with great peace. I knew that because Christ lived, I could face tomorrow. My Mother was only sixty-five years old, and I still miss her every day. But, I know I will see her again in heaven. I found that God, over time, does heal our broken hearts after loss and death.

As we stood by his hospital bed, my father who had Alzheimer's sang every verse of many hymns the night before his death. He also loved us to sing *Angels Watching Over Me.* At one point, he reached his hands toward heaven as if he saw others waiting for him. I believe with all my heart he did! My dad was received into heaven that very night. Death is real, but so is heaven!

I believe the hardest part about death is that no one can "fix" it. It is so final here on earth. But when you know Christ as Savior, you have a blessed hope of being with those loved ones again. Now, I rejoice in the heritage that both my parents have left, and I am focused on providing that for my children and grand-children. We all will experience the physical death of loved ones and even ourselves. The most important thing is that we are ready to meet our maker.

Was there ever a time that you confessed that you were a sinner in need of a Savior, repented of your sins, and accepted the free gift of salvation that He has offered to you through His death on the cross? He loved you so much that He took your place.

If not, you may bow your head right now and do so. I pray that you will. You pray something like this, but only in your own words:

> Dear Lord, I confess that I am a sinner in need of a Savior. I know I deserve nothing, but You died on the cross to pay the price of sin for me. You shed your blood that I might live for all eternity. I ask you right now to come into my heart, my life and save me. I want you to be Lord of my life. I thank you now that you have heard my prayer. Amen.

Here is what I would do next. I would write this inside of my Bible. "Today (write the date) I accepted Christ as my personal Savior." Then, sign your name. Whenever Satan comes to you to make you doubt, open your Bible, show him your signed name, and tell him to leave you alone because you want to live for Jesus. If you did what the Bible says to do, you may know you are saved. At the end of this book, I will put scriptures for you to know God's plan of salvation. It's the most important decision you will ever make in this life. No one is born a Christian; you must accept Christ on your own.

Now I would like to address another type of death of loved ones. It is the death through Alzheimer's Disease. This is what my sweet sister, Carol Ann, is dealing with now. This is like being with a living dead person. Right now, we do not know what they feel and think. My sister has gone downhill so quickly with this disease. It is so sad to watch and especially for her husband. They had so many plans for the "golden years." Many years ago, my sister accepted Christ as her personal Savior, and I know she will be in Heaven with a clear mind and we will rejoice together once again as we did before this horrible disease. Would you, along with me, find out as much about this disease and pray and give so that a cure may be found.

My Sister and Me in happier times

I thank God for resurrection through eternal life. As so the song continues...

And with your final heartbeat
Kiss the world goodbye
Then go in peace, and laugh on
Glory's side, and
Fly to Jesus and live!

Now, as I end this chapter and we go into the next one, I want to say this. Just as age, sickness, and disease can kill, so can phobias and fears. These types of sickness kill happiness and the ability to live life fully.

Chapter 6

Death of Phobias and Fears

I never thought that I would suffer from phobias. Flying was the only thing I was really afraid of doing. I flew home from college once and asked a very elderly lady sitting next to me if I could hold her hand on takeoff. She very graciously allowed me to do so. I felt so bad because her little hand was so fragile, and I was squeezing it with all my might. She never complained, and I often wonder now how that fragile little hand could have saved me.

There was a time shortly after Mother died that I went into deep phobias that continued for years.

I guess sometimes loss and grief can trigger this type of fear. The main one was agoraphobia, the fear of being out in open places. I remember traveling home from a conference in Dallas, Texas, and becoming overwhelmed by the feeling that I needed to get home! The outside world from the car was so big and scary to me.

I could hardly stand to be out and away from my home. Once, Bob and I were invited to visit friends who attended our church and were camping out at

Delaware State Park in Ohio. As we were driving out, I turned to Bob and told him that I needed to go back home. I was too afraid to go. He told me that we were halfway there, and it would take just as long to get there as it would to get back home. My breathing became difficult; my heart was beating out of my chest, and my mouth was dry. I said again firmly," I need to go home."

Even though he did not understand, he took me back home, called the couple, and told them we would not be able to join them that evening.

I felt ashamed, alone, and heartbroken. What was wrong with me? I could no longer go to the grocery store without feeling panicked and fearful that I would not be able to get out of the store. When driving, I would start out from my home then become paralyzed with fear and not be able to get back home. I would pull into a stranger's driveway and sit there until I felt I could go on again. A few times, I was almost home and could not drive over a small overpass. I would pull the car over and wait until I saw a car with at least one passenger, and I would flag them down and ask if one of them could drive me over the overpass in my car while the other drove over and met us on the other side. Not only was this embarrassing, it was also dangerous, because these people had to trust me, and I had to trust them.

I remember having a hard time going to church and had to sit in the back so I could make a quick exit if I felt fearful. Elevators paralyzed me also. What if the door did not open? Even now, just typing these memories is causing my palms to sweat.

The agoraphobia was coupled with panic attacks. Many times, I called my neighbor who lived a few doors down and asked her to come over because I thought I was having some type of medical emergency. Sometimes the emergency squad would come and check my vitals and knew it was panic. This was also brought on by extreme stress and fibromyalgia, which caused me great pain. It finally got so bad that I could no longer go out of my house to even walk to the mailbox. This is not good for someone who is in the public eye. I tried hard to hide all of this from my children. The fear, panic, and phobias went on for a few years. I could not sleep at night and tried everything I knew to do.

I remember one night listening to "Night Sounds" on Christian radio, and the announcer for the program, Bill Pierce, read Philippians 4:6.7 which says:

> Be careful (anxious) for nothing; but in everything by prayer and supplication with thanksgiving let your requests be made known unto God. And the peace of God, which passeth all understanding, shall keep your hearts and minds through Christ Jesus.

I had read those verses many times before, but that night, when I heard it on the radio program, it was like they jumped out at me; the ink was fresh. They were brand new, and it was those verses God used to help release me from my phobias and fears. Yes, that is the power of God's word. Now, I was not healed overnight but those verses became a part of me, and I quoted them over and over. I even set them to music.

I also sought professional counseling with a lady who would drive in the car with me. Then came the time when she would drive her car, and I would drive mine. She drove over the overpasses and waited for me. That way, I had to go over the overpass because I knew she was waiting. She also went into grocery stores and elevators with me.

Did you know that in a store, one reason you might feel trapped is the lighting and floors? The shiny floors reflect the lights and play tricks on your eyes. To avoid this, concentrate on objects as you walk up the isle toward the front door. Look at one object at a time. I share this because it really helped me. One more action that helped me overcome the fear was a rubber band that I wore on my wrist. Every time a fear came into my mind, I snapped the rubber band and replaced that fearful thought with a verse of scripture or an attribute of my Lord. It helped very much.

My husband really helped me; he became my supporter. It is so important to have someone with whom you feel comfortable who will give you leeway to turn around if you need to. After time went on, when I saw that he would stand with me, when I begged him to go back home and not go on, as he said, "okay," as he agreed, then I wanted to try to go on just because I knew he would understand me. Does that make sense?

Circumstances in life may bring about fear, panic, and phobias in your life as well, but be of good cheer because the Lord can heal that also. Do not allow these things to cripple your life. Listen for a verse you may claim as your own. Seek help as needed; there is nothing wrong with finding help, but do not linger in your fear. Even medication for a time is fine. My husband has diabetes, and he takes insulin. No one has ever condemned him for that. The brain is very intricate, and sometimes we need medication to help in time of need when there is a chemical imbalance or other illness. Those phobias and fears are dead to me now. Not that they will never come back, but I know the power of the word of God and who I am in Him.

"I sought the LORD, and he heard me, and delivered me from all my fears. This poor man (woman) cried, and the LORD heard him, and saved him out of all his troubles" (Psalm 34:4,6).

Seek the Lord and cry out to Him.

Here is another verse from "The Untitled Hymn" by Chris Rice

Sometimes the way is lonely
And steep and filled with pain
So if your sky is dark and pours the rain, then
Cry to Jesus
Cry to Jesus
Cry to Jesus and live

This hymn, written by Karolina W. Sandell-Berg also ministered to me for this is how I live, "Day by Day."

Day by day, and with each passing moment,
Strength I find to meet my trials here;
Trusting in my Father's wise bestowment,
I've no cause for worry or for fear.
He whose heart is kind beyond all measure

Gives unto each day what he deems best
Lovingly its part of pain and pleasure
Mingling toil with peace and rest.
Help me then in every tribulation
So to trust Thy promises, O Lord

That I lose not faith's sweet consolation
Offered me within Thy holy Word.
Help me, Lord, when toil and trouble meeting,
E'er to take, as from a father's hand,
One by one, the days, the moments fleeting,
till I reach the promised land.

The biggest lesson I learned through phobia and fears is that I really may trust the Lord. He has never failed me yet, and I know that He never will. God can do anything but fail, and He will not fail you, especially when you need Him most. He always knows just what we need.

Chapter 7

Death of Pain

I bet some of you turned to this chapter first. How do I know? Because we all suffer pain. You will not get out of this life here on earth without some scars of pain. I am talking about both physical and emotional pain. I have had my share of physical pain, especially with fibromyalgia diagnosed by a physician, and Meniere's disease, which is an inner-ear disorder. Meniere's causes extreme dizziness, and there were times I would fall onto the floor and lie there for hours simply because I was too dizzy to get up. I would lose my vision, and during one episode, I lost the hearing in my right ear, which has never returned. I even had an episode one Sunday while Bob was preaching, and I was sitting in the pew. Guess what? He never missed a beat of his message, and others attended to me. I am sure the stress of our home contributed to these pain issues.

My husband had this bright idea that since our kids were growing older (they were all thirteen) we needed to go across the country in an RV. So, he found an old

RV along the side of the road that he purchased for a small amount, and he began to fix it up.

The day came for the five of us to pile into the RV and head to Florida, to camp at Disney World, before we began our month-long journey across the US, headed to California to see his parents. This was during the time that I was having panic attacks and extreme pain from fibromyalgia. By the time we were heading back to Ohio, the RV had shrunk. It was so tiny that my three thirteen-year-olds (with all their teen emotions) had turned into monsters. Of course, I had turned into the Wicked Witch of the West with falling objects from the RV cupboards causing my fibromyalgia to worsen.

Down the highway we went. My husband was so anxious to get home, he literally drove seventeen hours straight to get us there. I am not lying when I say I had to pry his hands off of the steering wheel when we pulled into our driveway. It was a good trip, but one of those you kind of want to forget, especially the trip home. (Sometimes we must laugh after healing comes.)

Drink the Cup of Cancer

I have suffered the pain of cancer. I had to drink the cup of this disease when I was diagnosed with thyroid cancer. I was innocently washing my face before bed one night, and I discovered a lump on my neck. I showed it to Bob, and we agreed that it should be checked by the doctor. The doctor said it was suspicious and did a biopsy. When the results came back, they were inconclusive, so the physician decided to remove it.

Surgery was scheduled, and they took out the part of my thyroid where the lump was located. They sent it to be tested while I was still on the operating table, and it came back as non-cancerous, so they sewed me back up. After I came to from surgery, I was glad to hear the words "No cancer."

After a few days, I went home and was to return to my surgeon for a follow-up appointment in a week. Bob went with me. We were sitting in the room, and the surgeon came in, opened my chart, turned to me, and said, "Mrs. Burney, you have cancer." Then his pager went off, and he had to leave the room for a few minutes!

Bob and I looked at each other in disbelief. I thought the report was non-cancerous? What does this mean for me? I had never heard the word "cancer" pertaining to me before.

When the surgeon came back in, he said, "Yes, after further testing, the report showed a rare form of cancer."

They needed to go back in and remove the other half of my thyroid.

"What?" I said. "Don't you know I am the biggest chicken in the whole world?" It was all I could do to get through the first surgery, let alone go through another one within a week."

"God, what is it?"

But, as before, the Lord was with me. They removed the other half, and my recovery began again. Then, I started radiation. This was back in the '90s. They did things differently back then. I had to go into total isolation. They put up newspapers all over the walls of a hospital room down at the end of the hall. When I entered the room to begin my one-week stay, every-thing that I took in with me had to be thrown away before I was discharged. So, I took a small unmarked Bible, a couple of magazines, and some writing paper to write down any question or thoughts that I might have. I was served meals through a window on paper plates, cups, and I ate with disposable plastic silver-ware. Bob could not come into the room; He could only stand outside the door with a mask on for a short visit. When a nurse or doctor came in, they had on protec-tive gowns, gloves, and masks. I was radioactive.

The staff would bring me a pewter-type goblet, and I had to drink the medicine inside, which made me glow in the dark. Later, they would run a wand over my entire body to watch for any sign of cancer.

It was during this experience that I knew in some odd way what Christ might have experienced in the garden of Gethsemane. Remember when He said, "Father, if it could be possible, let this cup pass from me, Nevertheless, not as I will, but as Thou wilt?" It was by trust in my heavenly Father that I was able to drink the cup presented to me. You see, it was His will for me at this time in my life, and who was I to question what He wanted and needed to do in me. The cup which my Father hath given me, shall I not drink it? John 18:11

I love the song "Lead me to Calvary" by Jennie E. Hussey

May I be willing, Lord, to bear
Daily my cross for Thee;
Even Thy cup of grief to share,
Thou hast borne all for me.

Lest I forget Thine agony;
Lest I forget Thy love for me,
Lead me to Calvary.

Have you had to pray Jesus's garden prayer:
"Nevertheless, not as I will, but as Thou wilt"? From
what cup is it that the Lord is asking you to drink? Are
you willing or resisting? Before going into cancer surgery, the first time, I had to go up to my bedroom and
lay on my back on the bed. I was so scared to have surgery, so I decided to lay there and pray until the Lord
brought me peace. As I kept looking up at the ceiling
and pouring out all my fear and pain to the Lord, after
a time, it was as if the ceiling opened and the presence
of Christ came through to let me know that He would
supply my every need and be with me every moment.

Now some would say, "That is foolish." To them, I
answer, "Well, you were not in my bedroom."

God cares about our every need, and I don't know
about you, but I need Him every hour of every day. After
years of full-body scans, I am now cancer free. I continue to keep watch, but my Lord has been so gracious.

Years of Hell from Emotional Pain

During the time of my cancer, my father, who had
developed dementia, had come to live with us. My
father lived with us until we needed to place him in
an assisted-living facility. I count it a privilege to have
cared for him, however difficult it was.

Also, during this time, we were dealing with our
teenage son who desired the world's ways and was
experimenting with things we were not in agreement

with. I was caring for my first grandson who was born just five days after our son turned sixteen and teen girls who were going through struggles then and were extremely jealous and resentful of many things There was extreme anger in our home, and I had deep marriage problems with my husband. Bob and I were at opposite ends concerning how to handle all that was going on. We felt trapped in our home because one of us needed to be there due to circumstances beyond our control.

At one point, we even had a divorced lady who boarded a room in our home, which was actually not a good idea for us at this time. We also had taken in a troubled teenage boy. Once again, this was not the best decision for us at the time. Add to that all the girls and me under one roof who had our times of the month resulting in never a good day!

Me with Josiah. The Grand that gave me a reason for living

The one blessing in this mix was my first grandson. He was so innocent, and to this day, I really believe that his presence saved my life. That is why he is and always will be so extra-special to me. He was at that time, my reason for living. I am not saying I did not love my husband or children at this time; I just could not see that love between us then. We call it our years of hell because they were. Nothing was normal, all was in disarray, and it all took place in that piggish demon house.

This all weighed heavily on my shame-based personality. I wanted so much to do everything right, and yet all was going wrong. When I would act out during those years, I would walk away feeling totally embarrassed and ashamed. I sobbed many tears and kept wondering what was wrong with me.

No More Song

Music had always been a huge part of my life. When I was alone, I could sing all of my favorite hymns at the top of my lungs. Then, when others who conflicted with me came into the house, something welled up within me and the music was gone. I literally lost my song. I was a totally different person. There was so much anger inside of me, and I did not understand why.

To receive victory over life, I needed to get to the root of the problem. The anger that I felt from various life events and the issues that emerged from my learned performance-based acceptance were the root of what I needed to deal with in my life, but I did not choose to take action at that time. I was dealing with my problems selectively. Do you understand what I mean? We often pick and choose what we deal with, don't we? God wants it all surrendered to Him.

When my husband was very young in the ministry, he preached a message titled "The Sinful Apartment House." We laugh about the immature title now, but in reality, that is what I was living in through my lack of surrender. You see, I would surrender some of the rooms of my heart to God, but I kept other doors closed. No one could enter, not even God. How foolish I was. The Lord wants full access to our hearts. He wants nothing hidden, nothing between our soul and the Savior. God will continually show us areas of our life that are not surrendered to Him, and as He does, we need to listen and heed His call.

Parkside Experience

I remember wanting the whole family to go to counseling when we first adopted the girls. Our family grew from one to three five-year-olds overnight, and I did not want to fail as a parent. I felt like we all could benefit from counseling. The rapid growth of our family was both a great blessing and a huge responsibility. But, instead of the whole family, I was singled out as the only potential problem.

At one point during those years, I attended a day care at Parkside." The ad for this place said, "The healing begins the moment you call Parkside." I knew I needed healing from my fear of failure, so my husband would drive me out there to spend the day at least three times a week. Let me tell you, there was no healing at Parkside for me. At Parkside, I heard words that I had never heard before. It was a vulgar place, a place where a woman of God should not be, and I found no help there. It only made me feel more condemned.

When my husband arrived to pick me up, he could not understand why I was so angry. I was angry because of what I had heard and been around all day long and because no one was dealing with the root of my issues. (Even though I did not realize this at the time.)

The only help I found there was to help me end my dependency on Ativan medication. I had become addicted to it because of my panic attacks. A counselor had prescribed them for me and told me to keep taking them as long as needed. Now, let me say, being on Ativan to help with panic attacks was a good thing for me at the time. The bad part was that I got addicted to them. I actually could not get out of bed in the morning until I had taken one. I am thankful that God used Parkside to deliver me from the addiction, but that is the only reason. Isn't it amazing how we must sometimes go through a hellish situation to be released from a hellish situation? I give all glory to God because He works all things together for our good, even Parkside. "And we know that all things work together for good to them that love God, to them who are the called according to his purpose. For whom he did foreknow, he also did predestinate to be conformed to the image of his Son, that he might be the firstborn among many brethren" (Romans 8:28-29).

So you see, I experienced the death of emotional pain. There can be emotional and psychological pain in relationships whether it be with your spouse, your children, or so-called friends.

Friendships

All of us want to have friends. The Bible says that a man who wants friends must show himself friendly in Proverbs 18:24: "A man *that hath* friends must shew himself friendly: and there is a friend *that* sticketh closer than a brother."

Over the years, I have had many acquaintances, but not many close friends. Most of the things I have experienced in my life were not shared with anyone, friend or family. Part of the reason for my privacy was being in the ministry. When you are the pastor's wife, it is difficult to be really close to someone in the church. I had a few close church friends, but most of those did not really work out. Situations arose that divided the friendships.

Also, when going through a difficult time, people often do not want the friendship anymore because they do not want to be "involved" with someone who has a problem. I know that sounds strange, but it is true. A lot of times, false rumors are spread that cause the "so called friend" to withdraw and give their loyalty to the one or ones spreading the false rumors. I remember how it felt to be cut deep with a knife when I lost some "friends" from our church. Many times, it was the ones we had given the most help and time. Then, there is the loss of a "friend" at the time I needed their friendship most. I think I have experienced it all.

I also have had situations where I did not agree with someone on a particular issue, and while they said they were a friend, they pulled their friendship from me.

Isn't Facebook a wonderful tool? I have reconnected with so many of our young people from Wichita and

New Philadelphia. It is glorious! But have you ever been unfriended on Facebook? Now, it's not a good feeling. Talk about rejection! And we can become jealous and get upset over Facebook posts. It really brings out our un-crucified flesh, doesn't it? Sometimes, I do not think it is such a wonderful tool.

With the touch of a key, you are taken out of the loop as the person's friend. It is hard to understand, but at the same time it is hurtful.

Facebook is not the only way we may be hurt by friends or loved ones. Many times, we are betrayed. One thing that I have noticed in the times that we are now living, is that more people seem to want revenge in some way. People want to hurt someone in a way that would devastate that person. Somehow, it makes the one who is doing this feel better about themselves. With the age of cell phones, with cameras and video availability, it is easy to so-call "black mail" people who have wronged you. What if all our faults were on video or someone had a picture to use against us?

Yet, God sees all and still loves and forgive us. The Bible says, "Vengeance is mine, saith the Lord, I will repay" (Romans 12:19b). Why do we think we have to take things into our own hands? No one knows what God wants to do in those situations. Let's leave these matters to God, especially in friendships, church ministries, marriages, and so on.

The Value of a Friend

What is true friendship? Psalms 17:17a says, "A friend loveth at all times." I believe true friendship is somewhat like marriage in a sense. And I write "somewhat" and "in a sense." Obviously, marriage is in a holy category by itself, but in the Bible, you will note the deep friendship of Jonathan and David. A friendship should be for better or for worse. It is in sickness and in health. It does away with jealousy and envy. The Bible says, "Greater love hath no man than this, that a man lay down his life for his friends" (John 15:13).

Christ did that for us; He is the ultimate example of a friend. And He is called the friend that sticks closer than a brother. True friendship could also be described as family. But so much of that is dependent on what kind of relationship you have with your family. True friendships set aside fears and imaginations. True friendship esteems the other person better than themselves, like in marriage, and in some family situations.

"*Let* nothing *be done* through strife or vainglory; but in lowliness of mind let each esteem other better than themselves." (Philippians 2:3)

True friendship is a gift. If you do not have that type of friendship here on earth, make it a matter of prayer. God answered my prayers for a true friendship right after my sister started going downhill with Alzheimer's disease. I always knew that even though my sister did not live close to me, she would always be there for me. I really think she thought the same of me. If I had a special prayer request, I could call her and ask her to pray. If I just missed Mom and Dad, we could talk.

When her disease began to take over, she was no longer there. It was then that God brought a true friend into my life; and I am so thankful for her, especially in these later years of my life. I also had another true friend who moved away years ago. She was a pastor's wife too. I could call on her anytime, and she would be there. During some of my most difficult times, this lady would come to where I was, bring me a picnic-like snack, and just accept me for where I was.

Back then, it was so refreshing to me because I very rarely ever felt that anyone accepted and loved me just for who I was. God also gave me another friend who was there for me while I dealt with the overwhelming task of mothering three children all the same age. I used to think every battle was a hill to die on for what I wanted, but she helped me realize to choose only the battles that were really worth dying for.

I am sad to say, I did not always put her advice into practice, but that truth was always in my mind. These types of friendships are rare, and if you are blessed to have them, then cherish and nourish them. I believe we all need a friend or friends, but it takes work to keep a friendship going, just as it does a marriage or family relations. Do you have someone you could pick up the phone and call if that four in the morning call comes to your house, and you are devastated? We all need someone.

Here is another verse from "What a Friend We Have in Jesus."

Do thy friends despise, forsake thee
Take it to the Lord in prayer
In His arms He take and shield thee
Thou wilt find a solace there.

Walls of Pain

The shadow of death of emotional pain is something we will experience in various ways. I used to put up a wall. Not a real wall, but a wall just the same. I did not want to be hurt again, so I put up an invisible wall as a shield to keep others from getting too close to me. I believed that if anyone got close to me, they would see my flaws and not like me, or they would hurt me. When people who cared tried to approach me, they would see the wall, assume I did not want them in my life, and go away. That only made me think, *Well, see? They did not really want to be in my life*, and I would feel rejected. Hurts that happen throughout our life often cause us to build those walls. I also had built a wall with my husband through those "years of hell." There is a song by the Gaithers that says, "I built the wall one hurt at a time." Then the song goes on to say that He (God) healed the hurt one hurt at a time. I know the Lord did that for me. The wall has come down, praise God! Through the power of the word of God, I knew I was accepted perfectly and loved by the God of the Universe. I was then free to love and be loved by others. There is another Gaither songs that says, "I am loved; I am loved. I can risk loving you, For the One Who knows me best, loves me most."

I simply share my personal experiences, the perspective I developed through them, and how God gave me peace.

I have already shared some unusual situations, and now I will share one that took place years after the Parkside incident. This one had an unbelievable impact on my life. God used this event to bring to me the extreme brokenness He needed to perform in my life.

Broken: A Cry for Hope

1 Peter 4:12 says, "Think it not strange concerning the fiery trial which is to try you, as though some strange thing happened unto you." In the dictionary, the word trial is described as "the act or an instance of trying or proving" another word for trial is test.

Trials, we all go through them, even when we have so many reasons to be happy and content. Trials are a part of life. For the Christian, God uses the trials in our life to shape us into His image.

A W Tozer once said "It is doubtful that God can bless a man greatly until He has hurt him deeply." That sounds cruel doesn't it? But in my life, God's breaking of me was one of the best tools that could have ever taken place.

The following poem written by an anonymous poet speaks volumes of truth:

When God wants to drill a man,
And thrill a man,
And skill a man
When God wants to mold a man
To play the noblest part;

When He yearns with all His heart
To create so great and bold a man
That all the world shall be amazed,
Watch His methods, watch His ways!

How He ruthlessly perfects
Whom He royally elects!

How He hammers him and hurts him,
And with mighty blows converts him

Into trial shapes of clay which
Only God understands;
While his tortured heart is crying
And he lifts beseeching hands!

How He bends, but never breaks
When his good He undertakes;
How He uses whom He chooses,
And with every purpose fuses him;
By every act induces him

To try His splendor out
God knows what He's about

At this time in my life journey, I felt as if my life was shattered, and I didn't have hope. It was a very dark time in my life. Again, I cried out to God. This time, I simply asked for a reason to live.

Suffering from deep depression, with much turmoil present with my children and marriage combined, my emotional and spiritual health was totally broken down. My family of three teen children was broken; my marriage was ready to end. I was merely existing.

And then, *that day*! Yes, on *that day* my husband thought I was suicidal, so he took a drastic step and secretly called the police.

As I opened my front door to go to my car and leave for work, I saw many Westerville police cars in my yard, along with an ambulance. I was blocked in.

I did not understand, and as I walked over to my car, I thought, *Well, someone is going to have to move, so I may get out and get to work.*

I got into my car, but no one moved. Because I was so broken down emotionally, I thought, *Well, I might just have to back out. Surely they will move then.*

Instead of someone moving a vehicle for me to get out, my car was surrounded by four police officers, one at each door. I rolled down my window, and the officer there asked me, "Would you want to get into the ambulance?"

"No, I am leaving for work." I really thought it was a yes or no question. I found out that was the wrong answer. The police officer opened my driver's side door, reached in and grabbed me, and pushed me toward the ambulance. I had to get in.

I had no clue what was going on.

In the ambulance, the attendant asked me my name. Before I answered, I thought, "Well, my first name is Karen and middle name is Joy. No one had ever called me Karen, so through gritted teeth, I said, "My name is KAREN!"

And the ambulance took off and headed straight to the mental health portion of Riverside Hospital. As I was escorted into the hospital, there were armed guards by the door. Now I was really confused. The lady who questioned me for quite a long time said, "Well, right now, no one at home wants you there. Let's have you stay here with us for the night and have you talk to a doctor in the morning."

Those words resounded deep in my heart all that night: "No one at home wants you there." So, I was admitted. My goodness, what a shock! I have never stayed in a place where I could not have sharp items or items with cords or even mouthwash in my personal possession. I had to brush my teeth and comb my hair by going down the hall to a bathroom and have items given to me. I could not even have a belt on the robe they gave me.

Are you serious? I thought. *I have stayed in nice hotels and resorts with hair dryers in the room. I am not going to cause a problem.*

I was put into a room with a roommate, and I tried to talk to her. She made absolutely no sense, and being naive I did not realize she had been on drugs and was very confused. Here I was right in the middle of all of this.

Are you kidding me?

We had to attend classes during the day. For recreation, we got to walk down a few halls of the hospital as a group until we reached the outside door. This door led to a cement six-foot-high fence, and we were able to go out and walk in a circle to get a breath of fresh air.

Wow, really? What am I doing in a place like this, I am a wife, in fact, a pastor's wife. I am a mother, I am a college graduate... I was totally humiliated.

I saw the doctor the next morning and was diagnosed with very severe depression which also included episodes of Bipolar disorder. So, I stayed awhile, totally isolated from my husband and children, to adjust to the medication they gave me and try to heal. Now do you understand why hope was gone?

Upon my release, the nurse talked to me about going to a place for women or a safe house, but nothing was open. I had no other place to go, so had to go back home, but nothing had changed there.

I spent many nights driving around to avoid being in the drama at home, just as I had done before the hospital situation. On one night, before my hospital stay, I remember being so very lonely, hopeless, and despondent that I almost gave my soul away. Praise God that He intervened and protected me with His mercy. During this time, the song "Alabaster Box" became very dear to me. With all that I had been through, I may honestly say that you don't know the cost of the oil in my alabaster box. I just want to pour out my praise on the Lord. I cannot thank Him enough for His love and protection that evening. I am so undeserving, but He is so gracious.

Remember this quote by R. Zaccharias "Sin will take you farther than you want to go, keep you longer than you want to stay, and cost you more than you are willing to pay." Did you know that allowing your flesh to rule your life after your salvation is sin? Yes, it is. The Bible says that to him that knows to do good and does not do it, to him it is sin (James 4:17).

God had made provisions for me for these difficult days and situations, but I wanted to walk in my own strength and ways. You see, I wanted to do things my way. I thought I knew what was best for me. I thought I could change, heal, and fix myself and my problems. What I really wanted to do right then was to leave and begin my life again by myself. *Certainly, that would be a good solution. I would not have to deal with anything and could start fresh,* I thought. I was wrong. I totally ignored the riches I had in Christ right at my fingertips: His love, His protection, His provision, and His word. How foolish I was. In reality, my only hope was in God and His care for me.

One night, after I had been released from the hospital but was still avoiding my home, I was caught in a terrible winter storm, and I had to check myself into a local hotel to spend the night.

When I went to return home the next evening, the roads were so bad that I feared I would not make it home.

It was then that God stopped me in my tracks. It was as if I had hit a brick wall, but I had not. I came to a complete stop, and God convicted me that I needed to make a choice once and for all to either find my hope in Him or in others, circumstances, or this world's acceptance.

As this trial hammered away at me, huge chunks of my life came crashing to the ground. God brought me to the end of myself.

Christ spoke to my heart and said, "Joy, are you going to keep trying to go on in your own strength in your life, or are you going to go in My strength?" Now He did not say this audibly but in a still small voice to my innermost being. I swallowed hard. I knew I could not continue in my own strength, and I did not want to. I knew the truth of God's word and wanted only to have my life reflect Him. After all, since I was eight-years-old, God had been conforming me to His image through all that I had experienced. What a privilege that is. To think that the God of the universe desired me to be conformed to His image.

That night, I made a choice to trust Him in these trials and praise Him for He inhabits our praise. These scriptures are helpful to remember to praise the Lord in trials and suffering:

"Praise ye the Lord: For it is good to sing praises to our God; For it is pleasant, and praise is beautiful" (Psalm 147:1).

"But thou art holy, O thou that inhabits the praises of Israel" (Psalm 22:3).

"Rejoicing in hope; patient in tribulation; continuing instant in prayer" (Romans 12:12).

I believe the three key words for me in this trial were choice, praise and prayer. God was there to give me HOPE! The medication was now taking effect, and I was thankful.

Since the depression was so deep, the medication allowed me to process spiritual truths that I knew but had been too depressed to apply to my life. Often this is the case when you have a chemical imbalance. There is no shame in taking medication for whatever time necessary to help with this imbalance. Medicine is not the answer; the cross is the answer. Do not stay on medicine long, just long enough. Today, I do not take any kind of medicine as I did during that time.

I had been used of God before, but my own flesh and things of the world had blinded my eyes to the hope I have in Christ. But I knew if God used me before He could and would use me again!

Life circumstances had made me feel like there was no way out. But God knows; He loves, and He cares. Nothing can dim the truth of His word.

He is a good, good Father. He named all the stars and He knows my name. He calmed the storm, healed the broken hearted, raised the dead, caused the blind to see, and the deaf to hear. He never changes and He cares for me. He promises me in His word that I would not go through anything that would be too much for me that He would always make a way of escape. I fully believe that way of escape is through surrender to His ways.

I returned home and simply allowed God to transform my life once again before Him. I did not try to change others; I just wanted God to change me.

I asked God to work on ME, to show me His ways, to work His life in me and through me. I asked Him to heal me emotionally and spiritually as I made a choice to live ONLY in obedience to God.

God has healed me spiritually, physically and emotionally through the truth of His word and what was accomplished on the cross.

Let me testify to you that there is hope in obedience to God! There is hope in abiding in Christ. He is the healing Jesus Who will refresh, restore, and renew. And He is the God Who is able to do exceeding abundantly ABOVE ALL... and guess what?

Baby step by baby step (not all at once), God began to transform me; He lifted my depression and gave me the love I needed for life.

He also began to heal my marriage and family relationships. Bob and I have a life verse for our marriage. The reference is engraved in our wedding bands. The verse is Psalm 33:21 which says, "For our heart shall rejoice in Him, for we have trusted in His Holy Name."

Do you know that God's word is powerful and that He will do just as He says? The Lord restored our marriage little by little, and He gave us a love that we probably never thought possible. I am more in love with this man now than ever before. As I said, it did not come overnight, but God brought us to a place to trust Him again, and we greatly rejoice in His Holy Name.

And God continues to work in our family, and we will not give up! We have come this far by faith, trusting in His holy word.

Today, by obedience to God's truth, I walk in hope and victory for I know who I am in Christ; I am accepted, forgiven, loved, not condemned, His workmanship, seated in Heavenly places in Christ Jesus...

Now, here I am sharing this with you. I never thought I would ever mention this day in public BUT GOD did a work!

And now many weekends of the year through the CrossPower ministry that God gave to my husband and me, we go out to share the hope that only God can give through surrender to and abiding in Him.

I really believe that God birthed the ministry of CrossPower out of the brokenness He brought us through over the years. The principles of the cross that God taught to us as He was molding and shaping us are what we teach as we go out to proclaim the victory that is ours in Christ.

God reminded me of a song as I was traveling back home that snowy night. I will share the words with you.

I don't know what trial, testing, proving, or crushing you might be facing now; perhaps you have been in a deep depression, panic, pain or are downcast. I pray that you also will find HOPE again as I did, and then that you may also share that with others and tell them all our Hope is found in Christ alone!

I pray that these words and my experiences will help you remember that when hope seems far away, when darkness is your constant companion, there is safety under Our Lord's wings. It is He "Who comforts us in all our tribulation, that we may be able to comfort them which are in any trouble, by the comfort wherewith we ourselves are comforted of God" (2 Corinthians 1:4).

Here is the song God reminded me of on that snowy night. It is "Under His Wings" by the Ruppes. I feel that the Lord used this song to save my life. If you will, take the time to read the lyrics, you will see just how perfect it was for the situation I was in at the time. I pray this ministers to you.

My way was filled with danger. I felt alone
The enemy had singled me out to do me wrong
And when he drew near, my heart filled with fear
Then I heard my Friend, calling me to His side
And I ran under His wings
And there He covered me
And now I can sing
And the enemy still looks for me
But what he can't see is that I'm under my Lord's wings
Under His wings.

Thunder rolled, dark clouds were low
I was out in the storm
Shrivering in the coldness there
No safe retreat from home

And there were strong winds,
Would this be my end

Then I heard my Friend
Calling me to His side
And I ran under His wings
And there He covered me
And now I can sing.

And the storm still rages
But in the Rock of Ages
I'm resting safely here
Under my Lord's wings

Under His wings
Under His wings
Who from His love can sever
Under His wings
My soul shall abide
Safely abide forever.

I praise the Lord for this valley of the shadow of death, for it brought Life once again to me. Do you see? It is true; God makes all things new in His time just as this song by Diane Ball says:

In His time, In His Time
He makes all things beautiful in His time.
Lord please show me every day
As You're teaching me Your way
That You do just what You say
In Your time.

God's way is perfect and His timing is always right.

Chapter 8

Death of Perfectionism

"Please God, I am doing it right? Please, love me. Please God, I am trying my best. Please accept me. Please God, I want to do what is right. Don't punish me."

Perhaps you have said any one of these phrases or at least thought one or two. I had a warped view of God's correction of me. I knew God loved and cared for me, but I did not understand that His correction of me was not punishment. God chastised me for either correction or perfection, not punishment. There is such a difference.

When I finally learned and applied this principle, my whole life changed. I no longer worried about not pleasing God, but rather had a stronger desire to please Him because of all He had done for me. I knew that He accepted me perfectly in the Beloved, and I did not have to work, work, work to gain His acceptance, but instead I could work, work, work because I had His acceptance.

When you meditate on who you are in Christ, your whole reason for doing things changes. When you realize that He loves you perfectly, and there is nothing you could do or have done to make Him love you any-more, you see His love as overwhelmingly gracious. He is always working everything for your good. He always has your best in mind. He wants to conform you to the image of His Son, so He works all things together for your good. There is a verse in **1** John 4:18 that says: "There is no fear in love; but perfect love casts out fear: because fear hath torment. He that feareth is not made perfect in love."

For years, I thought that verse meant that if I could love perfectly, then I would not have to fear. One day, God revealed to me that I was not the one who had to have perfect love. I could not have perfect love, but my Heavenly Father has that kind of love for me. It is His perfect love for me that is able to cast out (eliminate) my fear! This changed me from the inside out. You see, God is righteous. That means in simple terms that He is always right! God will always do what is right for you and for your life. Whatever happens to you is not punishment, but correction or perfection so that He might conform you to His image and prepare you for your home in heaven as well as your life here on earth.

The things that happened to me early in life began in me a shame-based attitude. I felt shackled by failure and regrets if I could not produce performance-based acceptance. Because of this, I thought I had to prove myself to God and all those around me with a per-fectionistic lifestyle. Because of this mentality, I put unreal expectations on those around me including myself. I very rarely rested, because there was always something that needed to be done. It is not wrong to want things to be done decently and in order as the Bible says, but to carry it to an extreme is wrong. And when plans would not go well, I believed God was punishing me for not doing things perfectly. I know to you it might sound crazy, but it was truth to me. Does not even make sense, does it? But that is the flawed thinking of a physical and relational perfectionist.

I am so thankful that the Lord released me from perfectionism and that I now may relax and rest in Him. He is the only perfect One, and I may trust Him. He is the One Who said in His word that "*There is* therefore now no condemnation to them which are in Christ Jesus, who walk not after the flesh, but after the Spirit" (Romans 8:1).

I do not have to be perfect, in fact, I can't be.

I struggled so much with condemnation. If I messed up in any way, I felt condemned and extremely low (all of this was my imagination), and I would often lash out at those I loved the most. That is why the Bible tells us to cast down these imaginations: "Casting down imaginations, and every high thing that exalteth itself against the knowledge of God, and bringing into captivity every thought to the obedience of Christ" (2 Corinthians 10:5).

Condemnation and punishment were synonyms to me. If you did not like me, or if I failed you or messed up in some way, I felt it was my fault. I would beat up on myself, so to speak, verbally. For example, "I knew you could not do that. Why did you say that? You're not worthy." I did not realize the difference between condemnation, punishment, and chastisement.

One time, I spoke a church for a ladies night out. I was extremely tired as I was just returning from a trip to Florida and the event was in Ohio. I stopped by my house to change clothes quickly then out the door to the speaking engagement. After the ladies event, as I was driving back home (about an hour's drive), I was beating up on myself and thinking of all the things I might have said wrong or whatever. I was going right back into my shame-based, self-way of condemnation. When I arrived at our house and pushed the button to put up the garage door, my husband came out to greet me. Well, I really was not in the mood to talk to anyone. He began to tell me how someone had called and told him what a blessing I was to the ladies that evening. I did not want to hear that because I already knew I was a failure this evening.

As I went to get out of the car, I looked down. Lo and behold, I had on two different shoes. Not only were they different colors, but different styles also. One was open-toe, and the other was closed-toe. One was closed back, and the other sling back. At least they were the same height.

When I saw this, I ran into our bedroom and threw myself on the bed and began to sob. Bob left me alone. After a while, I realized what I was doing—diving back into the shame-based thinking. I knew that God had freed me from that, so I sat up, wiped my tears, and walked out into our family room. I then proceeded to tell my husband that if God used me in any way tonight, I would give Him all the glory and be thankful. I then smiled and thanked Bob for praying for me. It is hard work to rest in the Lord because we think it all depends upon us. How foolish that is. Hebrews 4:11 tells us, "Let us labor therefore to enter into that rest, lest any man fall after the same example of unbelief."

You see, it is hard work to rest from our own labors. We think we have to make it all work when God tells us to rest and believe what He is able to do in us and through us.

My perfectionism almost ruined me, my family, and those around me.

Oh, how I praise God for the death of perfectionism. Praise God, I serve a perfect Savior, and I may rest in Him.

Are you trapped in the perfectionism trap? If so, you too may be set free. Give it all up to Jesus and accept your acceptance in Him.

"To the praise of the glory of his grace, wherein he hath made us accepted in the beloved" (Ephesians 1:6). Accept your resurrection with Christ and take your seat in heavenly places. "And hath raised *us* up together, and made *us* sit together in heavenly *places* in Christ Jesus" (Ephesians 2:6).

Music has always been such a big part of my life. Here is another beautiful song that helps me remember to ask Jesus to fill me with Himself:

Jesus be Jesus in me
No longer me, but Thee
Resurrection power, fill me this hour
Jesus be Jesus in me.

Allow Jesus to be the perfect One in your life; He will do a much better job. It will transform your life. Maybe you are pride-based and think you can do things on your own. Then, accept your death with Christ, and allow Him to control your life. Die to your own control of your life. Remember what the word says: "For I know that in me (that is, in my flesh,) dwelleth no good thing: for to will is present with me; but *how* to perform that which is good I find not" (Romans 7:18).

Let Christ be your sufficiency. Take your place in both His death and resurrection.

Chapter 9

Death of Phony Self life

Oh, thank you, Lord, for the valley of the shadow of death of a phony self-life. The Bible says that in our flesh dwells no good thing, yet we often allow our flesh to rule and run our life. How foolish is that? When we walk after the flesh, instead of in the Spirit, we are phony. Years ago at a conference in Denver, Colorado, God showed me in a fresh new way Galatians 2:20: "I am crucified with Christ, nevertheless I live, yet not I, but Christ liveth in me and the life which I now live in the flesh, I live by the faith of the Son of God, who loved me and gave Himself for me." Right then, I realized for the first time that not only had I been saved from sin, but that Christ had also died to save me from myself. This was a life-changing moment for me.

At this conference with Chuck Solomon, I took ahold of and accepted not only my death with Christ but my burial and resurrection with Christ. Also, I accepted the fact that because of what Christ accomplished on the cross, I now had all the riches of Christ living in me.

Because of that truth, I was now able to live a consistent, victorious life on a daily basis as I surrendered to Christ in me. This was the time I came to the cross of Christ for my very life. I wanted my life to identify with His death, burial and resurrection. All a one-time work, but something I did not realize was daily victory was possible for me even living in this sinful world, not only in the sweet by and by but also in the nasty now and now! I wanted everyone to know this truth. Bob and I shared this truth while in Wichita, and again as we started the church in Ohio. I remember sharing this truth also with missionaries and watching it transform their lives.

In fact, it was this very truth that God used to call us to start CrossPower Ministries. Bob had been used of God in Africa to share with missionaries there on the victory that is ours in Christ. We knew that it was this message we needed to share with others.

So what happened to me later in my life during the difficulties with my children, marriage problems, and deep depression?

You see, I stopped choosing to put God on the throne of my life instead of myself. I did not allow Christ to work in me and through me to live the Christ life. God is perfectly capable of taking care of anger, depression, problems with others, fears, phobias, and temptations. My own flesh is not sufficient to do so. Do you remember what Paul in the Bible said he had to do? He said he had to take up his cross daily.

And he said to them all, "If any man will come after me, let him deny himself, and take up his cross daily, and follow me" (Luke 9:23).

What did they do on crosses? They put people to death.

In other words, Paul had to die daily to his self-life and instead embrace the cross of Christ. It is a conscious choice; one that needs to be made moment by moment, day by day. Eventually, it will become normal, like breathing in and out, but we will never do it perfectly until we reach heaven. So here on earth, it is always a conscious choice.

My self-life was put to death on the cross, and when I accepted Christ into my life, I was given His life. Old things were passed away, behold all things were new. God wants full control of my life, and He is totally capable of directing my life. When I give way to my flesh, I am in essence allowing that dead, stinky self to crawl out of the grave and control my life. I cannot emphasize enough that it is a daily choice of who we yield ourselves to, either God or our flesh. I also had neglected to apply who I was in Christ, which is an important part of accepting my resurrection. It's important to understand that depending on your personality type you will have more difficulty accepting either your death or your resurrection with Christ. A pride-based person will have difficulty accepting their death, and the shame-based person will struggle with their resurrection.

I constantly need to allow God to work in my life on a daily, moment by moment basis to show me His truth. Look in God's Word, and do a study on who you are in Christ. It will change your life as it did mine. Do you even realize how much pain I could have spared my husband, family, others, and myself if I had chosen daily to deny my flesh and self and accept who I am in Christ? You see, I was living the words found in Romans 7:19-25:

> For the good that I would I do not: but the evil which I would not, that I do. Now if I do that I would not, it is no more I that do it, but sin that dwelleth in me. I find then a law, that, when I would do good, evil is present with me. For I delight in the law of God after the inward man: But I see another law in my members, warring against the law of my mind, and bringing me into captivity to the law of sin which is in my members. O wretched man that I am! who shall deliver me from the body of this death? I thank God through Jesus Christ our Lord. So then with the mind I myself serve the law of God; but with the flesh the law of sin.

I wanted to do what I knew was right, and did in certain situations, but in other situations, I chose to ignore what I knew was right and gave way to my rotten flesh.

Do you ever do that? Everything you want to do are the things that you don't do, and the things you don't want to do are what you do?

Sometimes we find it easier than surrendering our wrong choices to God. It is often the easy way out but in the long run, it may cost us dearly. And so, like Paul the apostle, I had to say "O wretched man (woman) that I am!" And I had to realize again that Jesus Christ was the only One Who could set me free again. So I made the choice to embrace the cross.

Accepting the death of my phony self-life which Christ offered to me when He paid the price for me on the cross is another glorious death for me, and this same death can be yours as well. Accept your identity in Christ.

There is a song by Steve Green that we use as the theme song for our CrossPower Ministries. It is titled "Embrace the Cross."

I am crucified with Christ
Therefore I no longer live
Jesus Christ now lives in me **(in other words, identify with Christ's life)**

Embrace the cross **(make it yours)**, *where*
Jesus suffered
Though it may cost all you claim as yours **(you give up your rights)**
Your sacrifice will seem small beside the treasure
Eternity can't measure
What Jesus has in store **(His very life for you)**

Embrace the love, the cross requires **(His love is perfect)**
Cling to the One Who gave His life for you
An empty tomb concludes Golgotha's story
Endure then till tomorrow your cross of suffering

Embrace the life that comes from dying
(to sin and self)
Come trace the steps the Savior walked for you.
(He already walked it for you)

An empty tomb concludes Golgotha's story
(It is finished)
Endure then till tomorrow your cross of suffering.
(submit to God's molding of you)

*Embrace the cross. Embrace the cross, the
cross of Jesus.*

Chapter 10

The Peace of an Exchanged life

I am a very simple person. I lead a simple life. So for this chapter, I chose to make this concept of the exchanged life very simple. The exchanged life is one of the ways to describe living the Christ life.

What does it mean to exchange something? Well, if I buy something and it is either wrong or flawed in some way, I take it back to the store and exchange it for what is best.

Throughout my life, there have been many wrong or flawed emotions that I have displayed. These emotions were of my self-life, not the emotions of Christ. The emotions that I displayed at times when I acted out in anger were when I did not allow the beauty of Christ to be seen in me.

One of my mother's favorite choruses was "Let the Beauty of Jesus" by Albert Orsborn.

Let the beauty of Jesus
Be seen in me
All His wonderful passion

And purity
Oh, Thou Spirit divine
All my nature refine
Till the beauty of Jesus
Be seen in me.

Instead of allowing Jesus to be seen, I reacted in my flesh. Remember what Paul says about our flesh? In our flesh dwells no good thing. I know I have repeated this verse over and over, but I need to hear it. So why would we allow our flesh to rule our life; when God has made provision for us to live His life?

We often don't want to or refuse at the time to make the exchange.

Even now, if something goes wrong in my family, I feel ill. My heart gets very heavy, and I feel as though I have been kicked in the gut. I feel shaky and sad. It takes everything within me to turn to scripture and prayer and to make the exchange. It is easier to worry and fret. The promises of God are numerous, yet we resort to our fears.

The one particular promise of God for me is that He is the God Who is able. Able to do exceeding abundantly above ALL that we ask or think. Sometimes, all I can utter is "able, able, able." But I know He hears me, and He cares. The Bible says He keeps my tears in a bottle. The truth is God is at work even if I cannot see it.

God loves you as His child, and even when you don't understand or see His plan for your life, He is there, and He cares for you. You see, He wants the best for you and those you love.

I have recently come to the point in my life where I told the Lord, "I can no longer do it. I cannot fix everything. I cannot change anything. I am tired and weary. I want to just rest in the Lord. He does all things well, and He will do what is best. I will continue to delight in Him, look to Him in prayer, and trust Him to work. His Heart is for me, and His Heart is for you. Pour out your heart to Him for He cares for you. You matter to Him. What a relief and a burden lifter His love is, what a wonderful place of rest.

Take ahold of the promises of God, all of them are yes and amen. It is hard to choose to exchange because we would rather do it ourselves. Exchange all that you are not for all that Christ is. Bring your tattered rags to Him and watch Him make something beautiful. Whenever you make the exchange with Christ, you not only get what is good, you get what is even better, God's Best.

From as long as I can remember, I always had big dreams and hopes for family, ministry, and life in general. Over the years, many of those dreams crumbled right before my eyes. The best remedy that I took ahold of was wrapping those crumbled dreams in the rags of my life and laying them at the foot of the cross. The best reward was having Christ take those and allowing me to exchange them for all of His riches. My life is blessed by His fullness.

Another way to explain the exchanged life is illustrated in this song:

Not I, but Christ, be honored, loved, exalted;
Not I, but Christ, be seen, be known, be heard;
Not I, but Christ, in every look and action;
Not I, but Christ, in every thought and word.

Saved from my sin and myself, dear Lord,

Saved to be filled with Thee;
Self-crucified, so now not I,
But Christ, that lives in me.

This song was illustrated to me when I returned home from my hospital stay.

Determined to allow the Christ-life to overtake my life, I did not want to point out others faults and failures or point my finger at them to change. Instead, I had a deep desire to allow Christ to be Christ in me, and by doing so, allow Christ to change me from the inside out. That is the only way others may see Christ in you when your desire to live an exchanged life.

Oh, my friends, please fight for your life of victory. We are so prone to be a lazy people. Everything in our world today is for our comfort and ease. More and more daily tasks are made easier. That is good, but not when it comes to spiritual matters. Every day, we must go against the ways of this world and choose against our flesh. Every day, we must surrender to Christ all that is not of Him, and exchange it for all that He has for us. I really believe that in Heaven we will be surprised at all that could have been ours here on earth (spiritually) had we only yielded to His ways instead of saying, "Oh well, no one can live in victory." Yes, you can live in victory, because Christ has made that provision for you if you know Him as personal Savior. Some would look at my story and say something like, "Yes, just the typical story. She had all these problems and now she lives in victory, well good for her. But that is not normal! That is not how it is for the common, everyday person. The only reason for her is because she is in ministry."

No, nothing could be farther from the truth. God does not work in us according to our gifts, talents, stage, or position in life. He works in us because we are His children. He works in us according to His riches in Glory. He wants all to belong to us. His way is the normal way of life. The victory that He alone gives is the normal way of living. The way of our flesh is the typical way of this world. When we know Him as Savior, He gives us the opportunity to choose and to accept all that He wants to give to us. It is already ours as His child, but we must reckon it to be true and act upon the facts of scripture.

"Likewise reckon ye also yourselves to be dead indeed unto sin, but alive unto God through Jesus Christ our Lord" (Romans 6:11). There are two parts to this verse, dead and alive. So we must accept both our death with Christ and our resurrection.

This is not a "pie in the sky" existence. It is our normal inheritance by being a child of God, by accepting Him as our very own. The world's way is typical; God's way is normal. It is normal to have trials and shadows of death experiences on this earth but God will always bring victory when we obey Him.

You see, the war has been won, but we do face individual battles and many times we keep the battles going in our minds. Surrender your mind to Christ, only He is able to tear down any strongholds We might have individual battles, but victory has been promised us as long as we do it God's way. His way never fails. When Jesus cried on the cross, "It is finished' He meant what He said!

Chapter 11

Perfect Identity in Christ

Who am I?

"Danny, a name picked for a boy, but a beautiful girl must be named Joy!" As I said at the beginning of this book, these are words from a poem my mother wrote for me years ago.

Yes, they thought they were going to have a boy. Then, there I was, a daughter they named Karen Joy Forgan.

I like the name Karen, but my mother said that from the start they only called me "Joy." I remember when I started school, and they called the role on the first day each year, I never responded. As students, when our name was called, we were to stand and say "Present." That way our teacher would know we were there and could get acquainted with us. Every year, when the teacher said, "Karen Forgan," it did not register with me, because from the moment of my birth I was called "Joy." So I would just sit there in my seat. The teacher had to repeat the name emphatically louder, "KAREN Forgan!" Then, it registered, and I stood to my feet and

113

promptly answered, "Present, but could you please call me Joy."

Well, this name game continues to follow me all these years later. Now, not only am I legally Karen Joy Forgan who is really called Joy but I became (in 1969) Karen Joy Burney. I have at times been listed as Joy Forgan Burney. Some other names I have carried are daughter, sister, sister-in-law, wife, mom, and grandma. Other names I have had are student, teacher, pastor's wife, receptionist, friend, aunt, and cousin.

Year ago, I had to go to the hospital for an injury to my knee. While I was being transported in the ambulance, they asked my name. "Joy Burney." When I arrived at the ER, they asked to see my driver's license, which read "Karen Joy Burney." When I handed them my insurance card, it read "Joy C. Burney." *What? Where did that name come from? I had never seen that on my insurance card before.* Evidently, the insurance company made a typo and put my husband's middle initial down for mine since the insurance is through his name. So there I am, needing to be treated in the ER, coming in as Joy Burney, having a licensee that says I am Karen Joy Burney and insurance card that identifies me as Joy C. Burney; I have other legal papers that list my name as Joy F. Burney! No wonder they were going to reject me. I heard them say, "WHO is this lady really? Is this a case of stolen identity?"

Well, let me share with you who I am really! Several years ago, I established my identity. My identity is not in Karen, Joy, Forgan, Burney, not even in Joy "C." or in any of the positions I have had over the past years of my life. My identity is in Christ!

When I was eight-years-old, I realized that I was a sinner who needed a Savior, and I asked Jesus to forgive me and to be my very life. At that very instant, Christ took me out of the lifeline of Adam and placed me in the lifeline of Christ. In other words, He placed me "in Him." As the Bible says in 2 Corinthians 5:17 "Therefore if any man be in Christ,He is a new creature: old things are passed away; behold all things are become new." I became a new creature in Christ. I was given a new past, present, future, and name! Do you know how I like to refer to myself now? I like to say that I am "In Christ, Joy."

There is no confusion with this identity, and no one can steal this identity. Let me share with you just a portion of what this identity means to me. Because I am "in Christ":

I am accepted and loved. (Ephesians 1:6; Jeremiah 31:3)
There is no condemnation. (Romans 8:1)
I am free. (Romans 8:1-2; Galatians 2:4)
I have been given the righteousness of Christ. (2 Corinthians 5:21)
I am totally forgiven. (Ephesians 1:7)
I am seated in heavenly places. (Ephesians 2:6)
I am complete. (Colossians 2:10)
I am a conqueror over evil. (Romans 8:37)
I am chosen, holy, and blameless. (Ephesians 1:4)
I am redeemed. (Ephesians 1:7)
I have obtained an inheritance. (Ephesians 1:10-11)
I am sealed with the Spirit. (Ephesians 1:13)
I am alive in Christ. (Ephesians 2:5)
I am His workmanship. (Ephesians 2:10)
I am now light. (Ephesians 5:8)

I have been joined with all believers. (Galatians 3:28)
I am raised up with Christ. (Colossians 3:1)
My life is hidden with Christ in God. (Colossians 3:3)
I have been brought near to God. (Ephesians 2:13)
I am a member of His body. (Ephesians 5:30)
I have a bold, confident access to God.
(Ephesians 3:12)
I am always led in His triumph. (2 Corinthians 2:14)
My heart and mind are guarded by the peace of God.
(Philippians 4:7)
I am blessed with every spiritual blessing.
(Ephesians 1:3)
I am a son (daughter) and an heir. (Galatians 4:7)
I am a new creature. (2 Corinthians 5:21)
I am sanctified and justified. (1 Corinthians 1:2;
Romans 3:24)
My old self was crucified. (Romans 6:6)
I have all my needs supplied. (Philippians 4:19)

Oh, I want to shout: GLORY, GLORY to GOD! My identity in Christ can never be mistaken and never be stolen away from me!

You see, before I accepted Christ into my life, I was unholy, unrighteous, blemished, guilty, condemned, a prisoner on my way to hell and all the opposites of who I am in Christ. Satan would love to steal the identity that I have in Christ, but he cannot. I am protected in Christ, and no one or nothing can steal my identity. Now that is a real cause for thanksgiving and thanks living.

So, who is this lady, anyway? Let me tell you. I am:
In Christ,

Joy

Here is a song to illustrate. It is actually my testimony song titled "More So Much More."

Life had only begun when I gave Him my heart
(I was only eight)
Twas the dawn of that day, it was only the start
God's Law was satisfied
By His Son crucified
I was saved, was reborn in my heart

But there is more so much more than that
first sweet day
More so much more every passing day
I can be what I ought
In each deed in each thought
It's not I but it's Christ Who lives ***(Galatians 2:20)***

There's a peace in my heart which the world
cannot give
There is joy so much joy in each day that I live
For the life I now live
Christ is living in me ***(I have His identity)***
In each word, in each deed, each day

And there's more, so much more
Than that first sweet day
More so much more every passing day
I can be what I ought
In each word, in each thought
It's not I but it's Christ Who lives!

Here are some more words from "The Untitled Hymn"

Oh, and when the love spills over
And music fills the night
And when you can't contain your joy inside, then
Dance for Jesus
Dance for Jesus
Dance for Jesus and live!

I am dancing because I know who I am in Christ. Will you dance with me? My burdens have been lifted at Calvary.

But remember, this is a daily choice, and as I have said before sometimes a moment by moment choice. Satan does not want you to spill over to others with this message.

Do you wonder why more people do not come to Christ? I believe one reason is that they do not see a difference in us who are saved. We so often live just like the world in our actions, reactions, and choices. Like my mother always taught me: Dare to be different, and as the song says "Dare to be a Daniel, dare to stand alone. Dare to have a purpose true, dare to make it known."

Chapter 12

Purposeful CALL TO COMMITMENT

E verything that I have talked about in this book demands commitment. I would like to extend to you a "call to commitment."

Commitment means a total dedication and faithfulness to someone or something. It is a decision of the will, at a point of time. For example, giving God permission to have complete control of your life.Romans 12:1 reads: "I beseech you therefore, brethren, by the mercies of God, that ye present your bodies a living sacrifice, holy, acceptable unto God, which is your reasonable service."

In today's society, commitment has lost meaning and power.

Commitment is difficult. Only through Christ can we answer the call to commitment! We cannot do it in and of ourselves.

Commitment has to be something that makes up your life.

Christ wants us to keep on keeping on in our commitments and not faint. We are to be devoted.

Let me share with you today some commitments I have made in my life.

My first commitment was when I was eight-years-old. I accepted Jesus as my own personal Savior.

When I gave my life to Christ, I found a fulfilling relationship with God and an escape from the hopelessness of this world. Commitment is fulfilling. I want to be commited to ask Him each morning, "Lord, what would you have for me to do?" A hymn by Charles Wesley says:

"A charge to keep I have
A God to Glorify
Who gave His Son my soul to save?
And fit it for the sky!"

A second commitment was in junior high school when I committed my life to full-time Christian service. I knew that God's hand was upon my life, and I must be about my Father's business.

A third commitment was in 1966 when I went to Bob Jones University and graduated from there four years later. My parents sacrificed to give me this education, how could I do any less?

A fourth commitment came in 1969 when I married the love of my life.

Do you take this man to be your husband? Well, I just can't make up my mind. No, that is not the way it was.

I am committed to this man unto death do us part. Through the years, God has given us wonderful ministries to work in and blessing upon blessing.

A fifth commitment was in 1975 when I was introduced to the full message of the cross (death to sin and death to self and the exchanged life) through Chuck Solomon in Denver Colorado. This truth presented at this conference continues to change my life.

A sixth commitment was when in 1976, alongside my husband, we obeyed the call to begin a brand new church in Westerville. Ohio. Probably one of the hardest ministries we have ever done and yet so rewarding.

A seventh commitment came in 1978 when I committed myself to motherhood. My three children were born not under my heart, but in it. I could not shirk this responsibility.

An eighth commitment came in 1994 when I became a grandparent the first time. I believe we have a responsibility to pour our lives into our grandchildren and commit ourselves to them. I feel very blessed by my Grands through the years.

A ninth commitment came in 2001 when my husband and I committed our lives to begin CrossPower Ministries. We must get the message of the victory that was won for us on the cross to everyone who will listen. We told God we would go wherever He opened a door.

I believe God wants us to be committed to others by loving, praying, comforting, and edifying one another in honor, preferring one another.

Have you ever felt you are drowning spiritually? Like your faith is being sucked right out of you along with your hope, peace, and joy? Then, a committed member of the body of Christ comes alongside and breathes new life into you, encouraging you in the faith and you are restored, renewed, and ready to continue the spiritual journey? That is what happened to me in the friendships I talked about earlier. We are to bear one another's burdens.

We are to be committed to telling others about Christ and the victory that is ours through His sacrifice on the cross of Calvary.

We are to be committed to living the "cross" life. It is a life of sacrifice and obedience.

I believe Christ wants us to know that He is committed to us:

We will never perish.

We are never alone.

All of our needs will be supplied.

His love will never fail.

Just imagine what might happen if we would commit ourselves to knowing God through His Word and through choosing to live the cross life.

Conclusion

I want to conclude my book by sharing with you my own personal words in poem form that I have rewritten from a song I love called "Now More Than Ever I cherish the Cross" by Bill Gaither. I chose this because of my new understanding of the cross of Christ.

When I started this book in a faith like trust
I knew that the Lord's truth was best
I read in His Word how He cared for the birds
And knew when they fell from their nest.
Often I felt God's delight when I would do right
And I did not want to make my Lord sad
We communed thru the day from His Word, I would pray.
Oh, what sweet communion we had.

BUT now even more I treasure the cross
More than ever, I will share His Ways
All the years of my journey have shown my Lord faithful
As through the shadows of death I have passed.

All along hopes were dashed and dreams slipped by

But His promise of "fear no evil" was true
He was with me and held me and showed
me the way
And now, I share His Truth with you.

So now more than ever I treasure the cross
More than ever I look to His Word.
All the years of my journey have shown my
Lord faithful
As through shadows of death I have passed.

The shadows of death were conforming me to
The image of Christ all along
At times huge chucks of my life were cut off
And I stumbled for I thought I was wrong.

But God has been faithful to heal all my wounds and give to me rest in Him

Is the truth I have shared of consistent victory too good to be true?
I too found it hard to believe
You see, this old world has brain washed our minds
Into thinking victory cannot be ours.
So instead the hurt child inside us cries out
To be free and free indeed.
But the truth of God is real

And the Word of God says:

You are cared for
You are cherished
You are loved by God too
His sacrifice on the cross was for you.

Christ's death on the cross made it possible for us to be free and free indeed. We are able to make the exchange every day. All that He is for all that we are not. Now, I pray you see why, more than ever, I cherish the cross.

I want to live in the shadow of the cross.

I pray Christ is precious to you. He is the Mighty God and soon coming King. One day, every knee shall bow and every tongue proclaim that He is Lord. You may either bow the knee now and enjoy all of His provision for you, or you will bow the knee when He comes back, and if you have not accepted His free gift of salvation, it will be too late. Please exchange your life for His now. By the way, all that I have talked about in this book takes place at the time of salvation. It is just that for some of us (me) it took time to realize that all of this was mine!

It is so very important that we accept both the death of sin and the death of self. Christ died to save us from sin and from the self-life (our flesh). The death of sin is a one-time thing as we accept Christ as our personal Savior and ask Him into our life. The death of our self-life is a daily choice to reckon or affirm that it is so.

Oh, my heart's prayer is that you know Him and experience all the riches of Him.

Do I ever get angry anymore? Yes.
Do I ever get depressed anymore? Yes.
Do I ever feel lonely anymore? Yes.
Do I ever feel despondent anymore? Yes.
Do I ever get discouraged anymore? Yes.
Do I ever feel like quitting anymore? Yes.

If you have ever read biographies of some of the great servants of God, you will find many of them suffered from depression and exhaustion. Many would have to take time off to recover not just physically but emotionally from giving out with such fervency. I do not compare my life to those heroes, but it is true that we continue to experience all of the earthly emotions and must rest and refresh to continue to carry on for the Lord. The struggles in this life have been, are, and always will be real.

So, if I still at times have these feelings then what is different now? I now know how to deal with these feelings that come every so often. Even if you know the truths of the cross, you may lose focus. You might even take a plunge as I had done. What is true is that I cannot forget these truths. Once they were presented to me, I have a responsibility to live by these truths. The Bible says in Luke 12:48, "For unto whomsoever much is given, of him, shall be, much required." I must now realize that it is a daily choice. I take it to the foot of the cross, leave it there, and accept who I am in Christ. I give thanks and praise, and I tell it to Jesus through prayer. I exchange all that I am not for all that Christ is in my life. I die to my flesh, and I choose to allow Christ to live. In other words, I allow Christ to be back on the throne of my life again.

I trust Him to do the work in my life that needs to be done and to use me for His Glory. We are human and will never have total victory over these feelings here on earth, but God will always see us through and never fail us. And so I dance! And now, even as I continue my journey through the shadows of death, I am "Overshadowed" by His glorious love for me:

> *I'm overshadowed by His mighty love,*
> *Love eternal, changeless, pure,*
> *Overshadowed by His mighty love,*
> *Rest is mine, serene, secure;*
> *He died to ransom me from sin...*
> *He lives to keep me day by day.*
> *I'm overshadowed by His mighty love,*
> *Love that brightens all my way.*

All of us are different in the way we handle things, and circumstances in life will challenge how we handle ourselves. One thing is always true for those who have trusted Christ as Lord. This is the fact that we need to make a choice to allow Christ to be on the throne of our lives. He is the only One who is able to handle all that comes our way in this life. He and He alone is able to take you through the shadows of death so you may fear no evil.

My past, my present, and my future are in God's hands. I have experienced a blessed life even through the difficulties because Christ has used these valleys to pry my hands from this world and to allow Him to be my very life!

God's Plan of Salvation

We all know the ABCs. It is one of the first things we learn as a child. Here is God's plan of salvation for you using the ABCs backward.
The first is C, which stands for confess.
The second is B, which stands for believe.
The third is A, which stands for accept.

Confess Romans 10:9
"That if thou shalt confess with thy mouth the Lord Jesus

Believe Romans 10:9
"and shalt believe in thine heart that God hath raised him from the dead, thou shalt be saved"

Accept Romans 10:10
"For with the heart man believeth unto righteousness; and with the mouth confession is made unto salvation."

My Mother's Complete Poem for Me Pictures

To Joy

For quite some time now, I have been wanting to
write a poem just for you
I am lost for words to express
How much you have brought us happiness
For on Good Friday 1948
An angel opened heaven's gate
And God blessed us with another girl
We felt quite sure her hair would curl
Harry Jr, and Carol Ann waiting patiently
    For they wanted their little sister to see
A child dedicated to God from the start,
While Mother carried her under her heart
Danny a name picked for a boy
But a beautiful girl must be named Joy
Already you are almost at sixteen's door
It is good to remember the years that went before
From the beginning you won the hearts of everyone
It seems you are always so much fun
Singing, laughing and waving hi
To customers and passers by
When someone brought a toy for our young lady
It usually was a nice doll baby
Make room for the dolls and the stuffed animals too
No longer is there just a few
Deeply religious for a little one
Very early you know God's Son
And how He died on Calvary's tree
Giving His life for you and me
How can I this message to others bring
I am young but of Him I can sing
And for others you learned to pray
As you live for Him day by day

You start to school
And before long we know
Leadership qualities begin to show
It seems in so many things you are apart
Filling all the desires of your heart
Singing, speaking, whatever it may be
Doing these things making you very happy
Girl scouts, Y Teens, YF and Guild girls
We have now cut all the long curls
Many friends you have made in this little span
Continue on and do the best that you can
Your life you have given to Christ alone
And made His heart your sacred Throne
In these years you have met some trials
And have come thru and kept that smile
We have worked together in so many chores
At home, in church and here in the store
The blessings you have brought to our family
Can't be expressed in words, you see
And today this is our prayer
That you will keep your life in His care
Use your talents God has given you
Work hard and you will come thru
Your life is young, keep close to God
He will go with the paths that you trod
Do what you are called to do
Keep your faith, He will see you thru
With hopes and dreams and even fears of the morrow
Along with Christ we meet our joys and sorrows
You have your family always at your side
 And again I say, you have brought us much pride.
This day as I write this poem
With us you are still at home

Under the wings of father and mother
Other loved ones, a sister and brother
But as life goes on and you are on your own
I know you will remember the words of this poem
Written especially for our baby girl
And guess what, your hair did curl!
Mom

When we accept Christ as our Lord we pray the sinner's prayer. For example, "Lord, I know that I am a sinner but I know that Jesus paid the price for my sin on The Cross. I ask you now to come into my heart and be my Savior."

After salvation, when we realize we are doing things in our own strength (our self or our flesh), we need to pray the Selfer's Prayer.

Here is a sample prayer to pray concerning your self-life Composed by Dr. JohnWoodward of Grace Fellowship International and used with permission.

> I hereby surrender everything that I am, and have, and ever will be. I take my hands off of my life and release every relationship to You—every habit, every goal, my health, my wealth, and everything that means anything. I surrender it all to You.

And by faith I take my place at the cross, believing that when the Lord Jesus was crucified, according to Your Word, I was crucified with Him; when He was buried, I was buried; when He was raised from the dead, I was raised with Him. So I deny myself the right to rule and reign in my own life and take up the Cross and believe that I was raised from the dead and seated at your right hand. I thank You for saving me from my sins and myself. And from this moment on I am trusting You to live Your life in me and through me to do what I can't do and quit what I can't quit, and start what I can't start --that You might receive all the glory. I thank You now by faith for accepting me in the Lord Jesus, for giving me Your grace, Your freedom, Your joy, Your victory and Your righteous-ness as my inheritance in the Lord Jesus Christ. So even if I don't feel anything. . . I know that Your Word is true. . ., (I am) counting on Your Spirit to do what Your Word says. . . to set me free from myself, that Your resurrection life may be lived out through me, and that You may receive all the glory. I thank You and praise You for victory right now in Jesus' name, amen.

Note from the Author

I have lived a very satisfying life, fulling life, and I have experienced shadows of death. Shadows cannot harm you but they are able to scare you and cause you to stumble. They also hide the light. As a Christian our light is Jesus and we need to see Him. He is always there but sometimes we are in the shadow. Like a song I sing says, "Though sometimes I've stepped out of His will, I've never been out of His care." This book may not be what you expected. I trust, however, that the truth written in this book will have a positive impact on your life. If God is able to do all this for me, He is able to do the same for you. Please know that I appreciate each and every one of you. Thank you for taking the time to read my book.

In Christ,
Joy

This book is dedicated to my husband, Bob Burney

Thank you, Dear, for walking almost all of this road with me. Your teachings and unconditional love have ministered to me through the years. Your prayers lift me to the very Throne room of Heaven. Thanks for climbing over the wall and loving me. You have given me the courage to keep going in this life. I am blessed by the life and love we share.

I love you,
Your Wife, Joy

To those who have loved and believed in me no matter what, you have blessed my life.

Thank you,
Joy

Endorsement:

"My Shadows of Death is a book of the author's life and trials and troubles she faced.

It's always admirable to see an author willing to bare all when it comes to sharing hard times of life that are typically kept under wraps. However, in order to reach readers, and to potentially help them, authors need to be open with readers, which is arguably the biggest strength of this book."

Editor at Xulon Press

Notes

All song lyrics listed below are used by permission by the copyright holder

Chapter One
    Untitled Hymn – Chris Rice
Chapter Four
    Because He Lives – Bill & Gloria Gaither
Chapter Five
    Untitled Hymn – Chris Rice
Chapter Six
    Untitled Hymn – Chris Rice
Chapter 7
    Under His Wings – The Ruppes
    In His Time – Diane Ball
Chapter 8
    Jesus Be Jesus In Me – Gary McSpadden
Chapter 9
    Embrace The Cross – Steve Green
Chapter 11
    Untitled Hymn – Chris Rice
    More So Much More – Bob Oldenburg

CPSIA information can be obtained
at www.ICGtesting.com
Printed in the USA
FFHW02n1728061018
48715291-52764FF